The Blessing is in your Hands

W.E. CAIN

ACW PRESS

ACW Press
Phoenix, Arizona 85013

The Blessing is in your Hands

Cover design by David Chaney
Interior design by Pine Hill Graphics

Packaged by ACW Press
5501 N. 7th Ave., #502
Phoenix, Arizona 85013
www.acwpress.com

Printed in the United States of America.

ISBN 1-892525-45-3

DEDICATION

To my wife, Nancy for her support and patience. To Daddy's three little stars who shine so brightly in my life (Willie IV, Kyra Chantell and Ezekiel Elisha.) I love you so much. To my mother who gave birth to me and watched over the calling on my life. To my church staff and leadership without whom this book wouldn't be possible. Thank you for your dedication to the Lord and His servant. And finally, to all the family of Kingdom Church, who make it a joy to be a pastor.

ACKNOWLEDGEMENTS

To Bishop Paul S. Morton, my presiding Bishop for your humility and strength. To Bishop Dennis Leonard, my covering in the ministry, and Heritage Christian Center for their love and encouragement. To Bishop Larry D. Leonard for being a spiritual father and sharpening my skills. To Dr. John and Patricia Avanzini for teaching me the principles of financial prosperity. To Pastor Douglas W. Graves, my childhood pastor, for teaching me the foundational truths of who I am in Christ. To Pastor Rick Fox, my friend, for provoking me to thought on this project. To Pat Beshears and Kristi Phillips for smoothing out all the rough edges. To ACW Press for helping me give birth to my dream. To all of my family and friends in ministry. I am honored to serve with you all as loyal knights of the King.

TRIBUTE

AS I SIT HERE WRITING THIS tribute, it is the end of the book for me, rather than the beginning. I have written already what you will read after these pages. Although, I knew to whom I would write this book, I had no idea how I would be able to accurately articulate my feelings and thoughts. And although there are many for whom I am thankful; one specific person stands out in my mind, as a candle stands out in a dark room. I dedicate this book to my father W.E. Cain, Jr. He turned eighty years old on May 26, 2000. What can I say? Daddy, your love and compassion have taught me of God's grace and forgiveness. It has been your integrity and consistency through the years that has strengthened my faith in the unchanging character of God. The fact of the matter is, everything that I have learned about my heavenly Father came from your example, Daddy. You are such a great man. In all these years I never saw you angry. As I grew up, I would hear people speak so highly of you. Now that I'm grown, I still hear and see the love people have for you. I hope to be even half the man you are. Thank you for being everything that I ever needed in a father. Thank you for showing me how to be a father through your selfless life. I know that you have often told me how proud you are of me, but I want you to know…I need you to know, how proud I am of you. You are my hero, and I can say with confidence that I want to be like you because you are the closest example of Christ that I have ever seen. I am your Isaac and I know that after fifty-four years you finally got your boy. Because of the gap between our ages, I often wondered if you would even see my children, much less witness them grow up. I remember the day you calmed my fear. You looked at me with those loving brown eyes, rimmed by slight blue circles, and said, "Son, the Lord showed me that I would be around to see my grandchildren." And He fulfilled His promises didn't He Daddy? When I thought that you couldn't be any more wonderful, you showed me that you had more love in reserve. You are my childrens' delight and strength, as you have been for me all these years. Daddy, I don't know how many more years I have with you. I don't know which one will happen first, The Lord's coming or your home going. But, I want you to know that I love you with all my heart. Thank you for being there for me every time I needed you. I am more in love with the Lord Jesus because He blessed me with a father like you. The way I used to rub and kiss your bald head, my children are now kissing and rubbing mine. Daddy, you are the big eighty and I am only twenty-six. As you are walking deeper into the forest of the winter of your life, I am barely approaching the dandelions and daffodils of my spring fields. As I look over at you in your season, I can only pray that my life will have as much impact as yours has had, and be as peaceful and content with my winter when it comes. Nevertheless, as we walk this road, we walk it together. You on your side and I on mine, yet holding hands and walking in our purposes and individual seasons together. As I hold tight to that aged hand that has always been bigger than mine, I realize more than ever that truly, The Blessing…Is In My Hand. I love you Daddy.

CONTENTS

FOREWORD

In Pastor Cain's book, "The Blessing Is In Your Hands," he has taken the Word of God and shown us how we are blessed. The anointing that is on Pastor Cain's life will open your eyes and cause you to understand the provision God has made in your life like never before. He has shown us that we don't have to live in lack, but we can be blessed.

Pastor Cain has an insight to prosperity that will help anyone overcome the poverty of their past and trust God in a whole new way. You don't have to wait any longer, because the blessing is already in your hands.

Stop waiting for something to change in your life, apply the understanding of Pastor Cain's teachings and work your stuff. You have waited for your blessing long enough. As soon as you realize that the blessing is already in your hands, then you will realize that it is your time to be blessed!

Bishop Dennis Leonard
Heritage Christian Center, Denver, CO

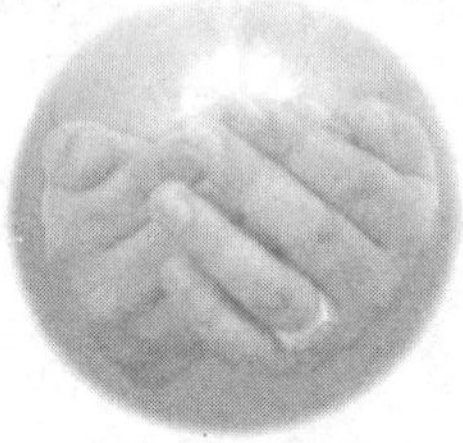

Lay not up for yourselves treasures upon earth, where moth and rust doth corrupt, and where thieves break through and steal:

—Matthew 6:19

ONE

I'm in the Will

IT HAS NEVER BEEN THE WILL of God for His people to go without and to suffer in lack. Throughout Old and New Testament dispensations, the Lord promised Israel, as well as the Church, that as long as they would serve Him, He would supernaturally supply every one of their needs. As we stand at the threshold of a new millennium, it is crucial for us to know our God as Provider, for no one else is our source.

> *Lay not up for yourselves treasures upon earth, where moth and rust doth corrupt, and where thieves break through and steal:*
>
> —Matthew 6:19

Jesus said, don't put your confidence in the economical structure of this world, because it all is subject to change. The stock market, Wall Street, banks and loaning institutions of every kind will fail. And when the bottom of the world's financial stability drops out, the only ones who will continue to prosper will be the children of the living God. We must first come to the realization, however, that God wants us blessed in every area of our lives. He desires us to be prosperous emotionally, spiritually, physically and financially. Actually, He wants us blessed even more than we want to be blessed. I didn't write this book to create an insatiable lust for money, but rather, to foster a proper understanding of your position and inheritance in Christ.

We are no longer outcasts, but now sons and daughters in His house. And the most exciting thing is that "we are in the will!"

> *The Spirit itself beareth witness with our spirit, that we are the children of God: and if children, then heirs; heirs of God, and joint-heirs with Christ; if so be that we suffer with him, that we may be also glorified together.*
>
> —Romans 8:16-17

Do you see what it says? You are a child of God, and as a child of God you have been made an heir. Everything that He has belongs to us. He willed it to us! Whenever a person dies and leaves behind assets and possessions, these assets are to be divided up by the executor of the estate. The way the executor assesses what belongs to who is by complying with the wishes and instructions of the deceased's last will and testament. Jesus died, but He rose from the dead. And when He ascended to the right hand of the Father, He placed the Holy Spirit, as the executor of His will and testament. God's word, the Bible, is His will and He gave us a new covenant: a New Testament that contains better promises.

> *But now hath he obtained a more excellent ministry, by how much also he is the mediator of a better covenant, which was established upon better promises.*
>
> —Hebrews 8:6

THIS BLOOD'S FOR YOU

Thanks be unto our Lord Jesus for making a way for us to come into the family of God. We are no longer outcasts, but now sons and daughters in His house. And the most exciting thing is that "we are in the will!" You are a beneficiary. Everything Jesus did was for us. Jesus didn't die for His sins because He did not have any. The stripes on His back weren't for His healing because He was never sick. He didn't provide financial abundance for Himself because at the Father's side He was never broke. The totality of His substitutionary work of Calvary was for you and me. He gave us a second chance. What Adam lost, Christ recovered. The blessing has been recovered and it's now your time to be blessed. Next time the enemy tries to discourage you, the next time he tells you that God isn't going to provide for you, grab God's word and tell him, "It's too late devil, I'm in the will." If God never wanted me to have it, then He shouldn't have written me in the will. It's out of my hands. The will and testament has been sealed in blood, the precious blood of the Lamb! You should take a minute, put this book down and wherever you are, begin to praise God for what He has promised you.

PUT UP YOUR DUKES AND FIGHT LIKE A SAINT

Be strong and of a good courage: for unto this people shalt thou divide for an inheritance the land, which I sware unto their fathers to give them. Only be thou strong and very courageous, that thou mayest observe to do according to all the law, which Moses my servant commanded thee: turn not from it to the right hand or to the left, that thou mayest prosper whithersoever thou goest.

—Joshua 1:6-7

God tells Joshua to be strong and of good courage as he is going into the land. The Lord had promised the land to Israel as an inheritance, but just because God had promised it didn't mean it was going to come easy. If you think your adversary is going to stand back and just watch you possess the land, you've got another thing coming. As a matter of fact, you might as well role up your shirtsleeves and get ready for a fight. Be strong and of good courage. Square your shoulders and encourage yourself in the Lord. When you feel like the enemy

When you feel like the enemy is gaining ground, just remember that your God told you to possess the land. Anything that is worth having is worth fighting for.

is gaining ground, just remember that your God told you to possess the land. Anything that is worth having is worth fighting for. Watch what Jesus says concerning spiritual aggression.

> *And from the days of John the Baptist until now the kingdom of heaven suffereth violence, and the violent take it by force.*
>
> —Matthew 11:12

Don't cower from your destiny any more. For this purpose you were born: to be blessed and to be a blessing. But, if you think that you don't have a right to be blessed, you will never be able to lay hold of it and help others to receive what God has for them. The Lord has sanctioned your breakthrough.

CHANGE YOUR MIND

> *And the child grew, and she brought him unto Pharaoh's daughter, and he became her son. And she called his name Moses: and she said, Because I drew him out of the water.*
>
> *And it came to pass in those days, when Moses was grown, that he went out unto his brethren, and looked on their burdens: and he spied an Egyptian smiting an Hebrew, one of his brethren.*
>
> —Exodus 2:10-11

I want you to examine, with me for a moment the story of Moses. God allowed Moses to be raised in Pharaoh's house because He wanted to reinforce Moses' identity and self-esteem. You see, if he had been raised like his fellow Hebrew brethren, he would have had the mentality of a slave, and a slave mentality can't lead anyone out of bondage. You need to change your mind about yourself, about your circumstances, about your finances, and say, "this isn't all for my life." How dare we act like lowly paupers when we are children of the King? Listen to what the embittered son said to his father when his prodigal brother returned home.

> *But he answered his father, 'Look! All these years I've been slaving for you and never disobeyed your orders. Yet you never gave me even a young goat so I could celebrate with my friends. But when this son of yours who has squandered your property with prostitutes comes home, you kill the fattened calf for him!'*
>
> —Luke 15:29-31 (NIV)

The older brother was saying, "Hey, I have been here. I have served you. I have paid my tithes, prayed, fasted, read your word and obeyed you like a good son and yet you haven't blessed me." But, now listen to what his father says to him.

> *"'My son,' the father said, 'you are always with me, and everything I have is yours.' "*
>
> —Luke 15:31 (NIV)

That should be enough to send you into a Holy Ghost fit. You have possibly been complaining about how you aren't being blessed. You have said, "I'm not prospering. It seems like everybody else is getting stuff except me." But, let the eternal words of your Heavenly Father echo through your spirit..."Everything I have is yours." What are you waiting for? You are waiting on Him, but He is waiting on you to embrace His promises. Don't let them go, no matter how hard the devil tries to pry them out of your hands. Hold on, don't give up. Be strong, don't get discouraged. Just remember, what God owns belongs to you. You're in the will! Everything that the Father owns has been given to His children. I just have one question. How much does God have? What does He own? In order for us to appreciate what God has given us, we must understand His ownership. Look at these scriptures and get ready to jump for joy!

"If I gave up my son, the treasure of heaven...don't you know I will give you everything that you need?"

> *The silver is mine, and the gold is mine, saith the LORD of hosts.*
>
> —Haggai 2:8

> *For every beast of the forest is mine, and the cattle upon a thousand hills. I know all the fowls of the mountains: and the wild beasts of the field are mine. If I were hungry, I would not tell thee: for the world is mine, and the fulness thereof.*
>
> —Psalms 50:10-12

Hallelujah! Do you understand yet? The Lord owns everything. I encourage you to stretch your faith like never before and begin to see a larger vision. When we view our need in the light of His inexhaustible supply, our need looks insignificant. God went to great extremes to bring us back into His protecting and providing arms. You are special to the Lord, and He was and is willing to do whatever it takes to recover you from the tyranny of the devil.

IT'S A PIECE OF CAKE

> *He that spared not his own Son, but delivered him up for us all, how shall he not with him also freely give us all things?*
>
> —Romans 8:32

This is the scripture I have been trying to get to for this whole chapter. The grammar of this text is a definite and emphatic question, the question that the Father asks us every time He sees us doubting His word. This is the question that He asks every time He sees us struggling in our fear. "If I gave up my son, the treasure of heaven…don't you know I will give you everything that you need?" In essence the text says, "It's a piece of cake." You need to get a revelation of that. "It's a piece of cake." Regardless of how hard your dilemma may seem, no matter how impossible your circumstances may be, to your Heavenly Father it is simply a piece of cake. He says He will freely give us all things. The phrase "freely give us" uses the Greek word ***charizomai, which means to grant as a favor, gratuitously, in kindness.*** Because He has given us His favor, we can enjoy all the blessings that He has made available to us. Look at all He has given to you. How can you be depressed when He has done so much?

Father, we thank you for the favor you have bestowed upon us. We thank you for everything that you have provided for us. We are your children, heirs of the promise. Thank you for putting us in the will!

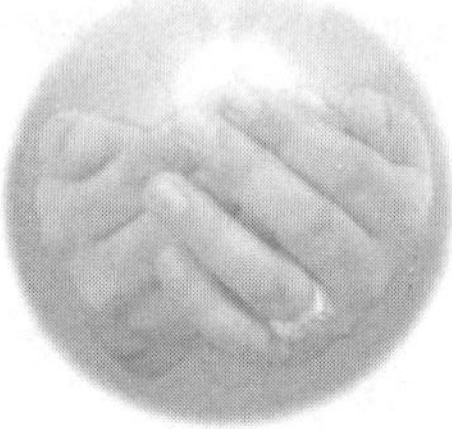

In the light of the king's countenance is life; and his favour is as a cloud of the latter rain.

—Proverbs 16:15

TWO

Nothing but Favor

And the LORD was with Joseph, and he was a prosperous man; and he was in the house of his master the Egyptian. And his master saw that the LORD was with him, and that the LORD made all that he did to prosper in his hand. And Joseph found grace in his sight, and he served him: and he made him overseer over his house, and all that he had he put into his hand. And it came to pass from the time that he had made him overseer in his house, and over all that he had, that the LORD blessed the Egyptian's house for Joseph's sake; and the blessing of the

LORD was upon all that he had in the house, and in the field. And he left all that he had in Joseph's hand; and he knew not ought he had, save the bread which he did eat. And Joseph was a goodly person, and well favored.

—Genesis 39:2-6

And Pharaoh said unto Joseph, Forasmuch as God hath shewed thee all this, there is none so discreet and wise as thou art: Thou shalt be over my house, and according unto thy word shall all my people be ruled: only in the throne will I be greater than thou. And Pharaoh said unto Joseph, See, I have set thee over all the land of Egypt. And Pharaoh took off his ring from his hand, and put it upon Joseph's hand, and arrayed him in vestures of fine linen, and put a gold chain about his neck; And he made him to ride in the second chariot which he had; and they cried before him, Bow the knee: and he made him ruler over all the land of Egypt. And Pharaoh said unto Joseph, I am Pharaoh, and without thee shall no man lift up his hand or foot in all the land of Egypt.

—Genesis 41:39-44

THESE SCRIPTURES ARE POWERful, but at the same time mind-boggling. I think I would have to say that Joseph is my favorite Old Testament character, for several reasons. He is the perfect shadow of the Lord Jesus Christ. There are so many similarities we should consider. He was a picture of Christ himself…a shadow. I won't exhaust all the ways that Joseph was a type of Christ, but can I take a few minutes and share a few things? These points might be worth remembering.

1. Joseph was the beloved son of his father Jacob. Jesus was the beloved son of His Heavenly Father.
2. Joseph wore a coat of many colors, and whenever they saw him wearing the coat they knew that he had the favor of the father resting upon him. When Christ was baptized by John, the Holy Spirit descended and rested upon Him. He's not just like his brethren. The anointing is the distinction.
3. When Joseph came to his kin, looking to be affirmed by his own brothers, they rejected him. Christ came to his own and they didn't receive him either.
4. Joseph was sold for 20 pieces of silver, Christ for 30 pieces
5. Joseph went down into prison. Christ went down into hell and preached to those who were in prison as ones being judged in the flesh.
6. When Joseph went down into prison he ministered to the butler and baker, one judged, the other delivered. When Christ died and desended, graves opened up all over Jerusalem.
7. When Joseph came up out of the prison, he did not have to work for the chain gang. Neither did he have to walk around convincing people that he was a reformed ex-con. He went all the way from prison to power. When Christ rose up from the dead, He held all power in His hands saying, "I am he who was dead and am alive forevermore."

8. When Joseph rose up he married a heathen woman. That Jewish boy took a gentile woman to be his bride. When Christ rose up from the dead, that Jewish boy also married a gentile bride and made her the Church.

Despite all these provoking and phenomenal things, there is still a strange element about Joseph: everywhere he went, and regardless of how hopeless it looked, he always had a tendency to rise up to the top. His brothers sold him to the Ishmaelites and he wound up in Potiphar's house. In just a little while, Potiphar positioned Joseph over all that he had. The rug was pulled out from him again and he finds himself incarcerated for something that he didn't even do. But, don't count him out because after two dreams and two interpretations, this ex-con becomes the Prime Minister of Egypt, accountable only to Pharaoh. There is only one word for these events, one word that explains what has happened in the life of this estranged Hebrew son. It's called "favor."

Some of us have thought that if we had more money we could accomplish the will of God, but it is not primarily money that we need.

The word favor means, ***to bow in the direction of the one being honored, to bestow kindness upon one who is unworthy and unexpected.*** Favor is a tangible force. God desires to release His favor in the lives of His people. Some of us have thought that if we had more money we could accomplish the will of God, but it is not primarily money that we are in need of. The missing ingredient is favor, because one day of favor is worth a thousand days of labor. You may have thought, "How in the world

> ***Favor is the key to the padlocked door. When everything that you have tried won't let you in, favor will open the door and roll out the red carpet.***

is God going to bless me with that job when it requires a college degree and all I have is a GED?" "How am I going to get that house when I don't have the down payment?" "How can I get the car of my dreams when my credit is 'tore up from the floor up'?" I don't care what the devil has barricaded against your blessing; when God bows in your direction, there is nothing that can stop the waves of favor that are coming from the arms of your Father God. Remember, favor is for the unworthy. So, if you think you deserve everything that God has done for you, then you aren't the one who will walk in this supernatural power called favor. Because if the truth be told, we have merited none of God's blessings in our life. The second qualification is "non-expectance." I call it the element of surprise. Just when you think it's not going to happen, God makes a way out of no way. Someone needs to know that favor is coming to your life. You weren't expecting the immensity of wealth and favor that are coming, but it doesn't change anything. Your breakthrough is in motion. It's already en route. Begin to confess the favor of God over your life. Favor will cause your enemies to be at peace with you. Favor is the key to the padlocked door. When everything that you have tried won't let you in, favor will open the door and roll out the red carpet. Look at what David the Psalmist said,

> *Thou shalt arise, and have mercy upon Zion: for the time to favour her, yea, the set time, is come.*
> —Psalms 102:13

Your appointment with God's favor has been scheduled. Don't envy people who are being blessed and don't murmur when you see someone receiving their financial harvest, because the Holy Spirit sent me to tell you that, "it's your time now!" All of heaven is applauding at what God is about to do in your life. If you murmur and complain you will short-circuit the power, but if you begin to praise God in advance, He will speed up the wheels of your destiny and usher you in to your breakthrough.

The last place that the Lord favored you was the last time you were obedient to His instruction.

The following are definitely not all the facts of favor, but are six of the most powerful ones.

1. Favor can make you rich in one day

In the book of Ruth you read the story of a Moabite widow who was remote from her homeland. Because of her commitment to Naomi, her mother-in-law, and the favor of God on her life, what Ruth could never have earned in a lifetime, she received in twenty-four hours. The Lord had already placed a Boaz in her path and this is what you have to conclude as well. There is a Boaz that God has released into your life, a person that is going to help you in the fulfillment of your God-given dream. For four hundred years the children of Israel were slaves in Egypt under the tyrannical reign of Pharaoh. Yet, in one day they came out with all the wealth of their slave masters and bankrupted Egypt. When you begin to declare the favor of God on your life, every day will present itself with the freshness of new possibilities. This could be the very day.

2. Favor can make you a household name overnight

Esther was an orphan in a strange land. Because of captivity, she became a refugee without identity or recognition. The king summoned all the most beautiful women of the land for the first beauty pageant, and out of hundreds, possibly thousands he chose her. A hateful, prejudiced king chose a Jewish bride and in one day she was a household name. A woman who had no name, no inheritance, and no destiny had now been called to the kingdom for such a time as this! One day she was a no-name, and by that same time the next day, she was the queen of the land. Likewise, out of millions of people, God will cause people to choose you because of His favor on you. You aren't going to have to hobnob, brown nose, or "get in good" with anybody to get what God has for you. Truly, He will cause people who never wanted to help you, open the door and welcome you with open arms.

It is obedience that got you here and it will be obedience that will keep you here.

3. Favor is birthed out of obedience, but is shut off when you deliberately disobey God's instructions.

> *If ye be willing and obedient, ye shall eat the good of the land:*
>
> —Isaiah 1:19

The last place that the Lord favored you was the last time you were obedient to His instruction. After the Lord had given Jericho into the hands of Israel, He warned them to continue to obey His instructions if they were to have permanent victory over their enemies. But, when they got ready to conquer the next city in line, Ai, the Bible says that they could not defeat this little, lightly-guarded city, because there was sin in the camp. Someone, somewhere had deliberately disobeyed the commandment and instruction that God had given and, as a result of the disobedience, the favor was turned off like a water faucet. If you are going to walk in the favor of God, you are going to have to learn how to carry out His instructions and to obey the voice of the Holy Spirit without hesitation or compromise. It is obedience that got you here and it will be obedience that will keep you here.

Whether you are a pastor, employer, or someone who has the power to help another to achieve their God-given destiny, when you show favor to someone, you are creating permanent job security for yourself.

4. *Favor is a seed that must be sown.*

> *Knowing that whatsoever good thing any man doeth, the same shall he receive of the Lord, whether he be bond or free.*
>
> —Ephesians 6:8

You have heard it said, "That which you make happen for others, God will make happen for you." The problem is, we are so concerned about getting ahead we don't have time to help someone else. But, if we would break the spirit of jealousy and self-centeredness, and begin to seed into other people's lives, we would soon see the harvest springing out of the ground of our generosity and humanity. While you are helping them, God is helping you. While you are pouring into them, God is pouring into you. And the more you give, the more is being given to you. I want all those in positions of influence to read closely now. Whether you are a pastor, employer, or someone who has the power to help another to achieve their God-given destiny, when you show favor to someone, you are creating permanent job security for yourself. Because, not only will they remember what you did for them, but God will record your act of kindness and favor and will carve out a permanent place in time for you. Don't be one of those who say, "I had to work hard for what I have, and I am not going to help anybody. If they want to succeed, they are going to have to do it like I did, the hard way." These people never open doors for anyone and they keep others in seclusion for fear that they will cease to be important themselves. But, if you will learn early how to favor others, and open doors for others, you will never cease to be in the game. Because, after your time to fight in the ring is up, God will reinvent you and make you the coach. Then, while others have retired and gone on to the convalescent home, you will still have a job, a destiny and an assignment in the game of life. Sow the seed of favor today, then sit back and watch the harvest that will spring up all around you.

5. *Favor is a lifestyle*

> *For his anger lasts only a moment, but his favor lasts a lifetime; weeping may remain for a night, but rejoicing comes in the morning.*
>
> —Psalms 30:5 (NIV)

The word declares that God is more intent on doing you good than He is on remembering your shortcomings. The word moment means a wink. In other words, before He can wink real good, His anger has passed. Oh, but His favor, it is for a lifetime! When His favor rests upon you, it is there to stay. Make up your mind that you are the favored of the Lord, and that you are going to walk through every door He is opening for you. Walking in favor is not a fad or a craze. You have to determine that it is for a lifetime. This is a lifestyle. Every day when you wake, as you get out of bed and lift your hands to stretch, through your yawn declare, "I'm walking in favor."

6. Favor will accelerate your destiny

Favor will shorten the distance of your journey. Regardless of how far you are from your intended destination, favor will shorten the mileage and bring you into that which you have been waiting years to see. In chapter eight, I will deal with this more in depth.

I mentioned earlier that favor can't be earned, but there is a way to position ourselves to experience God's favor on a daily basis.

PRAY IT ON DOWN

> *But seek ye first the kingdom of God, and his righteousness; and all these things shall be added unto you.*
>
> —Matthew 6:33

If we seek the Giver of the gift instead of seeking the gift, we will get the gift after all. It is important to realize that the closer we walk with the Lord, the greater His presence will be in our lives. Before you venture out into that dog-eat-dog world every morning, take some time to dedicate your day to God. You can't do this thing without Him. You can't be a good father without Him.

You can't be a good daughter without Him. You can't be a good employee without Him. You can't be a good boss without Him. In fact Jesus said,

> *I am the vine, you are the branches. He who abides in Me, and I in him, bears much fruit; for without Me you can do nothing*
>
> —John 15:5 (NKJV)

Whatever your task or profession, I guarantee you that if you'll spend time in the presence of God, the quality of your life will drastically change. Your promotion will come. Your raise will come. There is so much favor waiting for you.

Many times, I have witnessed the favor of God at work. Through the course of my life and ministry, I have witnessed time and time again the faithfulness of God. Although I could share testimonies that cite greater amounts of monetary or material blessing, there is a specific one that touches my heart the most, because it was in the earlier stages of my ministry. I remember it, as if it were yesterday. I was in a church service at Calvary Cathedral in Fort Worth Texas. I had gone there to enjoy the ministry of another evangelist who was preaching that night. While I was sitting there getting ready to give in the offering, the Holy Ghost spoke to me to give a seed of $100.00. Now, you might think that $100.00 isn't a lot of money, but at that time I was newly married, my first son had just been born, and we were living with my parents. We were struggling, and God told me, in a service that I wasn't even preaching in, to give $100.00. I sat there for what seemed an eternity, trying to reason with God. I was trying to explain to Him my financial predicament. But, what we fail to understand so many times is that our obedience is the breeding ground for miracles. After I finally resolved to give the amount that the Lord had instructed me to give, I began to write the check. As I began to fill in the amount of the check, a woman sitting behind me in the service tapped me on the back and asked if I was a preacher and what my name was. I confirmed that I was a minister and told her my name. I thought nothing of it, and really didn't pay it much attention at the time. As I proceeded to sign my name to my $100.00 check, this woman tapped me again on the shoulder and handed me a piece of paper saying. "Bless you." I thought, "how sweet," and placed it in my suit pocket. I gave what the Lord had told me to give that night and was extremely blessed by the service.

I went home after the meeting and, while I was changing out of my suit, I remembered the check that the dear sister had given to me. I opened it up and saw that she had written the check for $500.00. I began to weep and thanked the Lord for supplying our needs. But, the Lord spoke so clearly to me in the middle of my midnight and said, "If you would not have obeyed me to give what I told you to give, I would never have spoken to her to give you what you were needing." Let me stop and thank that sister, wherever you are. You will never know what you did. Not only did the Lord use you to help us in one of our greatest hours of need, but you also taught me a valuable lesson. The lesson was obedience, and obedience gives birth to favor. I encourage you, my brother and my sister, to stop trying to open doors for yourself and let the King bow in your direction. Because, when God affirms you, men will see and approve what God has approved. Stop fighting to get to the top. If you get yourself to the top then you will have to fight to stay there, but if God ever raises you up, you don't have to worry about staying there. He will ensure your success.

Father, thank you for being the awesome God that you are. You have been better to us than we have been to ourselves. When people ask us how we have come so far, we will say with humility and confidence, "It has been only by the Lord's grace and favor!"

And all the tithe... is the Lord's: it is holy unto the Lord.

—Leviticus 27:30

THREE

No Thieves Allowed

Will a man rob God? Yet ye have robbed me. But ye say, Wherein have we robbed thee? In tithes and offerings. Ye are cursed with a curse: for ye have robbed me, even this whole nation. Bring ye all the tithes into the storehouse, that there may be meat in mine house, and prove me now herewith, saith the LORD of hosts, if I will not open you the windows of heaven, and pour you out a blessing, that there shall not be room enough to receive it. And I will rebuke the devourer for your sakes, and he shall not destroy the fruits of your ground; neither shall your vine

> *cast her fruit before the time in the field, saith the LORD of hosts.*
>
> —Malachi 3:8-11

I AM AWARE THAT THIS IS A very familiar passage and possibly the most quoted scripture concerning tithes and offerings, but I would just like to take a few moments to underscore some things. As elementary as it may sound to some, we, as members of the body of Christ, are commanded by God's word to tithe our incomes into the kingdom of God. The tithe means the first ten percent. If you are not tithing and have no plans to start anytime soon, then stop reading right HERE. That's right, I said put the book down. Because, everything that is in this chapter and all of the proceeding chapters are written under the presumption that your tithe is being given to God. I am convinced that the reason why many Christians are not tithing isn't because they want to be in complete rebellion to God's word, but because they don't fully understand the principle and revelation of the tithe.

WAY BEFORE THE LAW

It is imperative that we first examine where the tithe originated. I have heard this argument many times concerning the origin of the tithe: "Well, that was under the law. God gave the commandment to Moses and we aren't under law anymore, we are under grace so tithing is outdated." But, bless those poor ignorant people's hearts. If you know anything about your Christianity, you should know that Abraham is called the father of faith. And, according to the word of God, Abraham was the first human to tithe.

> *Therefore it is of faith, that it might be by grace; to the end the promise might be sure to all the seed; not to that only which is of the law, but to that also which is of the faith of Abraham; who is the father of us all,*
>
> —Romans 4:16

We are his seed, his offspring. The law had not yet been instituted, but look at what father Abraham is doing:

> *And Melchizedek king of Salem brought forth bread and wine: and he was the priest of the most high God. And he blessed him, and said, Blessed be Abram of the most high God, possessor of heaven and earth: And blessed be the most high God, which hath delivered thine enemies into thy hand.* And he gave him tithes of all.
>
> —Genesis 14:18-20

God instituted the tithe in the Garden of Eden. It was there that He gave Adam and Eve dominion over all of His creation, but required one tree and commanded them not to touch it. When Abraham paid tithes, it was a sign of confirmation of the covenant that God had made with him. The Lord had promised Abraham that He would make him great and that He would bless him to be a blessing. There is something that we have failed to understand. The love of God is unconditional.

> *For I am persuaded, that neither death, nor life, nor angels, nor principalities, nor powers, nor things present, nor things to come, Nor height, nor depth, nor any other creature, shall be able*

to separate us from the love of God, which is in Christ Jesus our Lord.

—Romans 8:38-39

There is nothing we can do to disqualify ourselves from the love, mercy and compassion of God. But, when it comes to the blessings of the Lord in our lives they are not unconditional but rather conditional. Oh, yes. Look at these scriptures and see if you can notice the special word in these texts:

When true revelation is experienced, it is extremely hard to continue to live a lie, having tasted the reality of God's word.

And the LORD thy God will make thee plenteous in every work of thine hand, in the fruit of thy body, and in the fruit of thy cattle, and in the fruit of thy land, for good: for the LORD will again rejoice over thee for good, as he rejoiced over thy fathers: If thou shalt hearken unto the voice of the LORD thy God, to keep his commandments and his statutes which are written in this book of the law, and if thou turn unto the LORD thy God with all thine heart, and with all thy soul.

—Deuteronomy 30:9-10

Do you see it? The special word is "if." All through the word of God, the Lord has told His people, "If you do this, then I will do this." It is the initiation of covenant promises. The Lord established the perimeters of His blessing and favor. We cannot just live like we want to, and expect God to rain His blessings down upon us. He said, "If you follow my ways and uphold my statues then I will raise you up." I have heard a lot of different teachings on tithing over the years. Some of them were very good and others were left wanting true spiritual revelation. Through the years, I have seen that if you scare people to do anything, and they respond out of fear, it will just be a matter of time until the fear wears off and they return to living their lives in deception. When true revelation is experienced, it is extremely hard to continue to live a lie, having tasted the reality of God's word.

It is consistent tithing and giving of offerings that yield supernatural results.

EXCUSES, EXCUSES

There are many excuses that people use, not to tithe. One is, "That is Old Testament law and we are under grace." As we clearly saw earlier in the chapter, the formal tithe was instituted with Abraham. As a result of our faith in God and His son Jesus Christ, we are made children of Abraham.

> *Know ye therefore that they which are of faith, the same are the children of Abraham.*
>
> —Galatians 3:7

Another familiar excuse not to bring the tithe is, "I have so many bills, I just can't afford to tithe." This is the one that I have heard the most. What truly is being said is, "I don't trust God as my source of supply. I don't believe he can really take care of me." The tithe has always been an issue of trust in the mind of God. The Lord will never greatly bless someone that He knows cannot be trusted. So, we see then that the command to tithe is from God and must be obeyed.

WHEN WILL IT COME?

Many people have been discouraged in their giving because they didn't see immediate results. But, any farmer will tell you that it takes time for the seed in the ground to bring forth a harvest. It is consistent tithing and giving of offerings that yield supernatural results.

When we release our faith through the tithe, we untie His hands to work a miracle in our lives.

The enemy is counting on the fact that you will give up on God's economy. He is counting on the fact that, through discouragement, you will give up, and stop tithing and sowing seed. But, I have come to tell you, "don't give up now." You may have tried everything to get ahead in life. A self-help course...a financial freedom cassette tape series...a lotto ticket...an infomercial at three o'clock in the morning. But, don't you think it's time to do it God's way and see God's results? You might say, "If I tithe, then I will die of starvation or be thrown out of my house." But, I would rather be homeless and starving than to rob God. Because, if I have followed His command and been obedient, then He is obligated to bless me! What we fail to understand is that when we are robbing God by not paying our tithe, we bind His hands from blessing us. It's not that He doesn't want to; it's simply that He can't. Conversely, when we release our faith through the tithe, we untie His hands to work a miracle in our lives. In reading a recent report I was saddened to discover that less than eight percent of the body of Christ tithes. That means over ninety-two percent of the Church are non-tithers. It breaks my heart when I see churches struggling to pay the bills and keep the doors open. In most cases, it's not that the church doesn't have enough members or attendees. The reason why the financial needs of a church often times go unmet is that not even half of the local church is bringing in the tithe. Isn't that a shame? It is a shame for the simple reason that the Mormon Church is doing more in the area of evangelism than the true Church of the Lord Jesus Christ. Yet, within their organization you are not even recognized as a real Mormon if you are not tithing. If that were the standard of the Christian church, I wonder how many of us would be considered real Christians? (Selah) Please don't misunderstand. God does not need your money. The issue has never been one of our tithe taking care of the Almighty. You say, "then why is tithing not an option? If He doesn't need ten percent of my income then why must I give it?" That is a very easy question to answer. Look at the following scripture.

> *Lay not up for yourselves treasures upon earth, where moth and rust doth corrupt, and where thieves break through and steal: But lay up for yourselves treasures in heaven, where neither moth nor rust doth corrupt, and where thieves do not break through nor steal:* For where your treasure is, there will your heart be also.
>
> —Matthew 6:19-21

When we bring the tithe, we enter into relationship with God as His covenant partners. Our hearts are bonded to His presence, His purpose, and His kingdom when our treasures are with Him.

REVERSE THE CURSE

Another reason we must tithe is to release us from the curse we read of in Malachi's statement;

> *Ye are cursed with a curse: for ye have robbed me, even this whole nation.*
>
> —Malachi 3:9

We assume the curse to be God's active, personal judgment on us for not tithing. We've been taught that God, in a fit of displeasure, will strike us with a curse for robbing Him of the tithe. This teaching has been largely responsible for the fear and resentment most people have toward the whole idea of tithes and offerings! ***The truth is, the moment you devoted yourself to Him, all your possessions became "cursed"!*** Now, before you throw down this book, stay with me for just a few moments to see this amazing provision of God's Word! Notice this verse:

> *They shall eat the meat offering, and the sin offering, and the trespass offering; and every* dedicated thing *in Israel shall be theirs.*
>
> —Ezekiel 44:29

According to Ezekiel, all the tithes and offerings given to God were considered "dedicated things." The Hebrew word for "dedicated" is cherem (pronounced khay'-rem), and it refers to something captured, a doomed object, something cursed, devoted or dedicated. The spoil of Jericho was "cherem" to the Lord, as was anything dedicated to God (including land, houses, people, even your own body)! The idea of cherem is that anything devoted to God is under a ban to everyone else. If you keep it, tamper with it, try to sell it, use it, or hide it with your own stuff, you activate the curse *already on the object!* The only way to reverse the curse is to remove it from your stuff according to God's instruction. It's not that God will "zap" you if you don't tithe—the truth is that you are doomed UNLESS you do tithe. You have to give the accursed thing to Him to dissolve the curse!

If you keep it, tamper with it, try to sell it, use it, or hide it with your own stuff, you activate the curse already on the object!

Jesus demonstrated this principle on the cross:

> *Christ redeemed us from that self-defeating, cursed life by absorbing it completely into himself. Do you remember the Scripture that says, "Cursed is everyone who hangs on a tree"? That is what happened when Jesus was nailed to the Cross: He became a curse, and at the same time dissolved the curse.*
>
> —Galatians 3:13 (THE MESSAGE)

God doesn't want us to give Him the tithe to enrich Himself or to impoverish us — He wants us to get rid of the devoted/banned/cursed things so He can reverse the curse and pour out blessing in it's place! Hallelujah!

PREPARE FOR THE FLOOD

As I stated in the beginning of this chapter, the third chapter of the book of Malachi is the most quoted and prominent scripture referring to the tithe, but I am most fond of how the New International Version states this passage.

> *"…Bring the whole tithe into the storehouse, that there may be food in my house. Test me in this," says the LORD Almighty, "and see if I will not throw open the floodgates of heaven and pour out so much blessing that you will not have room enough for it…"*
>
> —Malachi 3:10 (NIV)

All of our lives we have heard that God would open up a window of heaven and pour out the blessings. If the Lord just opens a window, I might be able to contain the blessings that flow from that window, but if He throws open the floodgates, then He will drown me in my blessing. If you haven't been tithing, I encourage you to make the decision that will change your life forever. If all you have been experiencing are little drops of provision, little prosperity drips, why don't you change your membership? You may ask, "My membership?"

Yes, change it from the cursed club to the tithers club. Aren't you tired of not having enough? Always having to struggle to survive? There is a better way. There is a place of abundance that is waiting for you to enter into. Oh, but let me remind you, NO THIEVES ALLOWED. Today is the day to decide to come out of the wilderness of spiritual and economical famine and put on your scuba gear because the wheel is being turned and the floodgates are beginning to open right now. See your miracle gushing out from the throne of God. Open up your mouth and tell the Lord, "No more drip-drops…drown me in your presence, power, and provision!"

HIT THAT DEVIL WHERE IT HURTS

Honor the LORD with thy substance, and with the firstfruits of all thine increase: So shall thy barns be filled with plenty, and thy presses shall burst out with new wine.

—Proverbs 3:9-10

Oftentimes we rob ourselves of the richness of a particular text when we fail to go into the original meaning. I appreciated this passage of scripture far more after I saw what it was really saying; I think you will as well. Look with me at these particular words, and let's see what their meaning is in Hebrew.

Honor—Kabad—severe, numerous, causatively (heavy in weight)

Substance—Hown—riches, wealth

First fruits—reshiyth—the first in place, time, order or rank

All thine increase—tebuwah—total income, produce

So now by knowing what each individual word means we can grasp a greater understanding of the text. The literal translation then would be,

"Get severe, numerous in your giving...be a heavy weight when it comes to blessing the Lord with your finances. Give out of your wealth, and when you give to Him, give Him the first,

the prime, not the leftovers...of all your income, produce and revenue."

The devil should have never let you pick up this book and read it, but oh well, it's too late now. If he has ever been scared of you, he is right now, because there is a champion in your spirit. There is a heavy-weight champion within you and through your tithes, offerings and obedience to the word of God, you are going to knock the enemy out, and walk away with prize in hand!

Lord, we are going to give you the first fruits of everything. Because it is the first that determines the rest. Today, we break the hold that fear had on us. And we decide that we will be consistent and faithful tithers. Thank you Lord for giving us the opportunity to prove you in this.

And she said, As the LORD thy God liveth, I have not a cake, but an handful of meal in a barrel, and a little oil in a cruse: and, behold, I am gathering two sticks, that I may go in and dress it for me and my son, that we may eat it, and die. And Elijah said unto her, Fear not; go and do as thou hast said: but make me thereof a little cake first, and bring it unto me, and after make for thee and for thy son. For thus saith the LORD God of Israel, The barrel of meal shall not waste, neither shall the cruse of oil fail, until the day that the LORD sendeth rain upon the earth. And she went and did according to the saying of Elijah: and she, and he, and her house, did eat many days.

—I Kings 17:13-14

FOUR

The Prophet's Reward

And it came to pass after a while, that the brook dried up, because there had been no rain in the land. And the word of the LORD came unto him, saying, Arise, get thee to Zarephath, which belongeth to Zidon, and dwell there: behold, I have commanded a widow woman there to sustain thee. So he arose and went to Zarephath. And when he came to the gate of the city, behold, the widow woman was there gathering of sticks: and he called to her, and said, Fetch me, I pray thee, a little water in a vessel, that I may drink. And as she was going to fetch it, he called to her, and said, Bring me, I pray thee, a morsel of bread in thine hand. And she said, As the LORD thy God liveth, I have not a cake, but an handful of meal in a barrel, and a little oil in a cruse: and, behold, I am gathering two sticks, that I may go in and dress it for me and my son, that we may eat it, and die. And Elijah said unto her, Fear not; go and do as thou hast said: but make me thereof a little cake first, and bring it unto me, and after make for thee and for thy son. For thus saith the LORD God of Israel, The barrel of meal shall not waste, neither shall the cruse of oil fail, until the day that the LORD sendeth rain upon the earth. And she went and did according to the saying of Elijah: and she, and he, and her house, did eat many days. And the barrel of meal wasted not, neither did the cruse of oil fail, according to the word of the LORD, which he spake by Elijah.

—I Kings 17:7-16

He that receiveth a prophet in the name of a prophet shall receive a prophet's reward; and he that receiveth a righteous man in the name of a righteous man shall receive a righteous man's reward.

—Matthew 10:41

For whosoever shall give you a cup of water to drink in my name, because ye belong to Christ, verily I say unto you, he shall not lose his reward.

—Mark 9:41

I HAVE BEEN LEERY OF WRITING this specific chapter. I do not want it to be misunderstood by people who have been hurt and abused by professed men of God who have financially raped the people of God. Through the years, I have seen things said and done in the name of God that possessed neither the heart nor the character of God, and individuals ended up getting hurt and taken advantage of. But, I have also seen people so scared that the man of God has anything, that they would rather him live in nothing, drive nothing, and have nothing. I liken the minister and the ministry to a messenger and a camel on a long journey, who share one canteen of water. If the camel (ministry, church) drinks all the water, then the messenger (minister, pastor) will die.

Then, though the camel arrives at it's destination, it arrives with no message, because the messenger died of thirst. On the other hand, if the messenger gets all the water and the camel goes without, then the messenger might survive, but the camel will die and the messenger will be stranded, unable to deliver the message. So it is when a church is being blessed and the pastor is taking all the monies. The carpet in the church is shabby yet the pastor's house looks like The Taj Mahal. All of the other leadership is looking broke, busted, and disgusted, but he looks like he just stepped out of GQ magazine. The church has to do fish fries to keep the lights on, while he has more gold on his fingers than Fort Knox contains. But, what about when the church is being blessed and the finances are doing well, but the man of God and his family go unattended?

If the headship is blessed, then everything under the headship, by divine order, must prosper.

He is struggling to pay his bills, while trying to get a word from God for the people. It ought not to be this way. He is embarrassed to go anywhere because of the inadequacies of his clothing. Your pastor should be the best-dressed, because he reflects God. And not only does he reflect and represent God, he represents you. He should be blessed and prospering. Why would you want it any other way? As the head goes, so goes the body. Blessings are directional. That means they come in a certain direction and they go in a certain direction.

FROM THE HEAD DOWN

> *Behold, how good and how pleasant it is for brethren to dwell together in unity!* It is like the precious ointment upon the head, that ran down upon the beard, even Aaron's beard: that went down to the skirts of his garments; *As the dew of Hermon, and as the dew that descended upon the mountains of Zion:* for there the LORD commanded the blessing, even life for evermore.
>
> —Psalms 133:1-3

If you notice, the oil was poured on the head but it ran down. The place of blessing is under the head. If the headship is blessed, then everything under the headship, by divine order, must prosper. You never see a river flow upstream. The flow is always downstream. So, the place where you want to be is submitted to your leader. You want him to prosper, because as soon as he gets his blessing it's just a minute before yours is coming. As a matter of fact, if you really wanted yours, you would be campaigning for the man of God to get a new car and stop driving that hunk of junk. You need some more wheels, but you can't even get a window to open.

This Sunday you should to hand him a love gift and let him know, "Pastor, I am sowing this seed into your life because I am wanting to ensure my blessing." I guarantee you, if you will begin to attend to the man of God's needs, God will attend to yours. The story of Elijah and the widow of Zarephath is a particularly interesting and powerful one. The first thing to notice is that God was sustaining the prophet at the brook of Jeraphath, and the ravens were bringing him food. There is something that you must understand, and that is, whatever God orders He always pays for. Where there is vision there will be provision. What we must realize is that God always takes care of His servants who are in His will. So, when the brook dried up, God sent Elijah to this widow, both to sustain Elijah and for him to pronounce a prophet's reward blessing over the widow and her son. God had put her in Elijah's path to be the instrument through whom He would work to sustain the prophet. Notice that Elijah didn't ask her to sow into the church. He didn't ask her to give what she had to the ministry. He said, "Bake me a cake first." God will never elevate you above the level of blessings experienced by your spiritual head. David knew, even as a shepherd, the importance of an anointed and prosperous head.

God will never elevate you above the level of blessings experienced by your spiritual head.

> "*...thou anointest my* head with oil; *my cup runneth over.*"
>
> —Psalms 23:5

A Middle Eastern shepherd knows that there is great importance in anointing the head of the sheep. The anointing flows from the head all the way down into the wool and down to the hooves of the sheep. This would make it easier for the sheep to slip out of dangerous circumstances. The oil would also serve as lubrication for tight spots on the journey and would act as a healing balm if the sheep should fall and cut itself, the saturation of the oil into its body would protect it from infection. This is the reason why, when you are plugged in and connected to your head (pastor, leader etc.), a powerful anointing is released. These are things that you would not have been delivered from had you not been connected. Now you will slip right out of the trap the enemy has laid for you. And when it seems like the enemy has hemmed you in, the lubricating effect of that anointing will cause you to push your way through when others are being trapped. I grew up believing that the preacher was simply there for the people; to do what they wanted him to do, when they wanted him to do it and how they wanted him to do it. It wasn't until later that I began to learn that the office a man or woman of God holds is one of honor. Please understand, I think one of the most revolting things to see is preachers who have their nose so far up in the clouds that if it were to rain they would drown. Yes, a man or woman of God should possess a spirit of humility and be grateful that God has consented to call them. At the same time, the people must understand

Change the spiritual climate of your life by giving into the life and ministry of your man of God...your prophet, and get ready for your prophet's reward.

that the minister is a gift of God, given to the body of Christ, not to be abused nor taken for granted, but to be appreciated and honored.

> *Let the elders that rule well be counted worthy of double* HONOUR, *especially they who labour in the word and doctrine.*
>
> —1 Timothy 5:17

The word Honor in this particular passage of scripture is the Greek word "time" (tee-may') that means, "a value, i.e. money paid, or esteem (especially of the highest degree). I have heard individuals say right here, "Well, he is fine because he makes a salary from the church, or ministry, and that is all he needs." But, how do you put a price tag on an eternal gift? And who are you to determine the ceiling of blessings and finances that the Lord has ordained for His servants? One of the greatest principles you can learn is that the characteristics of the kingdom derive from the king. Show me how a pastor is living and I will show you how the church is living. If the pastor is always under financial burdens, more than likely the church is experiencing the same difficulties. If the man and woman of God are being blessed, the majority of the people under that ministry seem to walk in favor and provision. So, I challenge you today to change the spiritual climate of your life by giving into the life and ministry of your man of God...your prophet, and get ready for your prophet's reward.

> *Father God, thank you for our leaders. Show us this week how to be a blessing to them. Let them feel our sincere appreciation for their*

dedication and sacrifices. We are determined to receive a prophet's reward so we will begin to be a blessing in the lives of the men and women of God whom you have placed over our lives.

Owe no man any thing, but to love one another: for he that loveth another hath fulfilled the law.

—Romans 13:8

FIVE

No More Debt

However, there should be no poor among you, for in the land the LORD your God is giving you to possess as your inheritance, he will richly bless you, if only you fully obey the LORD your God and are careful to follow all these commands I am giving you today. For the LORD your God will bless you as he has promised, and you will lend to many nations but will borrow from none. You will rule over many nations but none will rule over you.

—Deuteronomy 15:4-6 (NIV)

HE WILL BLESS YOU AS HE *has promised!* Notice, He said that He promised to bless you. He gave his word to provide for you and your house. It is not only God's will for you to be blessed, but also to be free from debt. It is not the will of the Lord for you to have mountains of debt that you cannot see past.

When you are in debt, you are no longer working for yourself, but for the person that you are indebted to.

He said that you would lend to many nations, but you would not borrow. The Lord doesn't want you to be in a state of borrowing because whomever you owe, you are in one way or another enslaved to. You may say, "I'm not anybody's slave!" But just think of it, when you are in debt, you screen your calls because of the collectors.

When you are in debt, you are no longer working for yourself, but for the person to whom you are indebted. That is the reason why the Apostle Paul tells us,

> *Owe no man any thing, but to love one another: for he that loveth another hath fulfilled the law.*
>
> —Romans 13:8

You have been on the receiving end, but God says; "I want to turn the tables in your life." I want you to be the one who is lending. I want you controlling circumstances and situations. The root of continuous debt is greed. If the enemy can keep us in a vicious cycle of greed, we will never get out of debt. Instead of always wanting what someone else has, always needing more and never becoming content with what God gives. If we are going to walk in a place of supernatural supply, we must first begin to appropriate wisdom in our finances. One major lesson we need to learn as the people of God is: if you can't pay cash for it...don't get it. I know that we have heard that before. Far more credible men than I have given us that advice and we have been foolish not to take heed. Great men of God have written books on how to get out of debt. Books like, *Rapid Debt Reduction* by Dr. John Avanzini, *Money Cometh* by Dr. Leroy Thompson, and many others. This chapter is not to walk you through the step by step process of how to get out of debt, but to motivate you to start today. For debt will stunt your financial freedom. The Lord might be blessing you greatly. It might not even be an issue of your needing more money; it could just be that you need the money you have freed up and not going out each month on bills for things that you really didn't need.

If we are going to walk in a place of supernatural supply, we must first begin to appropriate wisdom in our finances.

The Lord has made you the head and not the tail. You are above only and not beneath. We have been trapped by the commercialism of this society and we have been competing with the Jones for so long that we have ignored the hole it has torn in the fabric of our family life. We have made the mistake of allowing materialism to be the measuring stick of our happiness. It's time for you to take your life back into your own hands. That is the

We have made the mistake of allowing materialism to be the measuring stick of our happiness.

reason why I believe that as we go into the twenty-first century, you and I are going to begin to see a tremendous number of Christians becoming very successful entrepreneurs. It's time for the children of God to own their own. There is transference of wealth that is happening. No longer are millions and billions of dollars going to be in the hands of the Bill Gates or the Donald Trumps of this world. The Lord says He is going to put creative and witty ideas in the hearts of His people who are going to bring in multiplied millions of dollars in order to fund His final harvest of souls. I have just one question. Why not you? Why can't you be one of those whom the Lord is going to use to finance the kingdom of God in this last and final hour? I believe you are. I believe right now, as you read this book, the Holy Spirit is stirring greatness within your spirit.

The Lord is going to put creative and witty ideas in the hearts of His people who are going to bring in multiplied millions of dollars in order to fund His final harvest of souls.

He is giving you the ideas, the concepts and the inventions that will usher you in to the place that He has for you. It is within you. The Lord placed it there. He said,

> *Remember that it is the Lord your God who gives you the power to become rich. He does this because he is still faithful today to the covenant that he made with your ancestors.*
>
> —Deuteronomy 8:18 (TEV)

Do you hear that? You've got the power! You have what it takes to be that millennium millionaire whom God is raising up. He said that He gave it to you, so He might establish His covenant and maintain His faithfulness to you. This gospel of the Kingdom must be preached in all the world...then the end shall come. We are delaying the coming of the Lord Jesus by staying in debt, and in dead-end-jobs that cause us to worry more about our bills than about the souls of lost men and women. The Lord has sent me to you today to shake you loose from the strongholds and chains of low thinking and under-achieving. You may have said, "I don't have what it takes to start my own business and be successful at it. I don't have the needed education or the talent or the time." All of that very well may be true, but you have overlooked one very important point: You've got the power!

COME UP AND SEE

We cannot even begin to comprehend, with our finite minds, the purpose and plans that God has laid out for His people. Look at what He told Isaiah:

> *For my thoughts are not your thoughts, neither are your ways my ways, saith the LORD. For as the heavens are higher than the earth, so are my ways higher than your ways, and my thoughts than your thoughts.*
>
> —Isaiah 55:8-9

Our problem has been that we have limited the Lord's ability in our lives because we have reduced Him to a mere man. We have given Him limitations and have told Him what He is, and is not, capable of doing. We have forgotten His absolute attributes. It is impossible for God to fail. It is not within His composition to fail and neither can He lie. Notice, I didn't say He doesn't lie. He cannot lie, because if He ever lied it would become the truth. He compares His way of thinking so absolutely higher than ours. God has a way of doing business that very few men have learned. The world says to cheat and con. God says to be a person of integrity, to be honest and open. The world says to climb the corporate ladder and step on whomever you have to, to get to the top. But the word says to prefer others above yourself. We have to begin to renew our minds to the way that God conducts His business. Come up higher in your thinking. We must strive to know, and to live out of the Master's heart. He has spoken concerning you and your welfare. He has shared his thoughts about you.

> *I alone know the (thoughts) plans I have for you, plans to bring you prosperity and not disaster, plans to bring about the future you hoped for.*
>
> —Jeremiah 29:11 (TEV)

Right there wherever you are, take the limitations off your powerful Jehovah Jireh and let him begin to blow on the embers of greatness within your spirit. You do have what it takes to come out of debt. You do have what it takes to provide for your family. You do have what it takes to be financially independent. You do have what it takes to finally achieve your dreams.

> *Hallelujah! Daddy God, you are our Jehovah Jireh. We thank you for helping us get out of*

debt. We refuse to be slaves one more day. We boldly confess, "We are debt free and in a better place to be a blessing to others."

And Joseph dreamed a dream, and he told it his brethren: and they hated him yet the more.

—Genesis 37:5

SIX

The Dream Maker

For God speaketh once, yea twice, yet man perceiveth it not. In a dream, in a vision of the night, when deep sleep falleth upon men, in slumberings upon the bed; Then he openeth the ears of men, and sealeth their instruction,

—Job 33:14

HAVE YOU EVER HAD AN IDEA? Have you ever had a plan or a thought that seemed unattainable? Let me just set your mind at ease and let you know that it very well could have come from God. Job said that God speaks in dreams. He went on to describe dreams as "night visions," or visions that are seen at night. There are some visions that the can only be seen and birthed in the night. If you have ever gone through a dark place in your life, when you thought you would never see or feel the warm sunshine again, then you know what I'm talking about. There is a night that will cause you to shake from the cold, bitter wind. There is a night in which the darkness will engulf you to the point that you can't see your hand in front of your face. There is a night in which your friends turn their back on you and you seem left and forsaken. But, that is when the dream comes. A dream can sustain you through experiences that should have killed you.

A dream can sustain you through experiences that should have killed you.

Now Israel loved Joseph more than all his children, because he was the son of his old age: and he made him a coat of many colours. And when his brethren saw that their father loved him more than all his brethren, they hated him, and could not speak peaceably unto him.

And Joseph dreamed a dream, and he told it his brethren: and they hated him yet the more. And he said unto them, Hear, I pray you, this dream which I have dreamed: For, behold, we were binding sheaves in the field, and, lo, my sheaf arose, and also stood upright; and, behold, your sheaves stood round about, and made obeisance to my sheaf. And his brethren said to him, Shalt thou indeed reign over us? or shalt thou indeed have dominion over us? And they hated him yet the more for his dreams, and for his words.

—Genesis 37:3-8

In all that Joseph went through, it was the dream which kept him alive through all the vicissitudes of his life. He couldn't die or get discouraged, because it wasn't what God had shown him. Likewise, God has shown you some things for this new season in your life, and you cannot give up. But, can I share a little advice with you that might help you when it comes to the dreams, and the things that God has spoken into your spirit? Don't tell your dreams to just anybody. Not everybody wants to see your dream come to pass and, if the truth be told, some would like to see you fail before they see you succeed.

A friend of mine, who grew up in Texas, calls this the "Crawdad Principle." When you catch "crawdads," or crawfish, you don't need to cover the bucket as long as one crawdad can't reach the top on its own. You might think that, with a bunch of crawdads in the bucket, they would crawl over each other until some could reach the top and crawl out. The truth is, however, that as soon as one crawdad begins to rise above the others, all the other crawdads around it begin to grab its legs and pull it down! They will grab, pinch, pull and fight to keep any of their own from making it to the top, instead of working together to achieve their freedom! Joseph's brothers acted out the "crawdad principle." They hated and resented him because of the dream he had about them bowing down to him. You have to be

You need to get a vision for your life that looks so big that you know that the only way for it to come to pass is for God to do it.

careful with whom you share your dreams and visions. You can't expect everyone to want you to live out your dreams, because that might involve their position changing in your life. They might not be able to control you anymore.

But, you have to determine that you aren't going to live out anyone else's dream for you; that it is now time to dream your own dream.

SLEEPWALKING

> *"Here comes that dreamer!" they said to each other.*
>
> —Genesis 37:19 (NIV)

Have you ever heard people say that about you behind your back or under their breath? Here comes Mr. Faith, or here comes Ms. Crazy. If you are going to see the manifestation of your dream, you have to learn how to spiritually sleepwalk. That is to say, you have to learn how to continue to walk by faith, even when people are criticizing your dreams and you don't see the outcome of what God has shown you.

> *(For we walk by faith, not by sight:)*
>
> —2 Corinthians 5:7

What we often don't understand about our adversary is that his main form of attack in our lives is not one of advancing against us, but of opposing and stopping our progress. If the enemy can cause you to stop for long enough, he can sabotage and thwart your victory. Therefore, you cannot stop. You have to learn how to continue to walk by faith, even as you pass people who are laughing at you. You must walk on even when you have no one who will walk with you. And though there will be those who say, "Oh look, here comes the dreamer," don't let that be all they say. Make sure they also say, "Hey, there *goes* the dreamer." You can't depend on intellect, or explanation, to guide you to your desired end. For, you have to stop trying to see where only your faith has been authorized to go. Put your faith behind the wheel, so that when you are stopped at the gate and asked where it is that you are going, you can simply point at the driver and say, "I'm just riding with him." You need to get a vision for your life that looks so big that you know that the only way for it to come to pass is for God to do it. There is no requirement to exercise faith in matters in which you can see and understand now, when, and where it is going to be done. You have to grab hold of the hand of faith, while faith grabs hold of the hand of God, and follow the dream (vision). Joseph's brothers didn't accept his dream because they had not seen it. Don't be upset with them. God had not revealed it to them. And, so it is with you, don't be upset with those who can't understand your dream. God didn't give it to them, he gave it to you.

It is only when we yield to His skillful hands, and trust in His power to do in us that which cannot be done by us, that we will see the manifestation of the desires of our heart.

> *Delight thyself also in the Lord; and he shall give thee the desires of thine heart.*
>
> —Psalms 37:4

All my life, I have heard this passage of Scripture quoted and for years I had no idea what it really meant.

I just thought the Lord was saying that if I would delight in Him (whatever that meant), He would give me the things that I desired. Until I understood the revelation of this text, I was a frustrated Christian. I was frustrated because I thought I was delighting in the Lord and I didn't understand why He was not honoring my desires and making what I wanted happen. You may have asked the same question, so let's take a deeper look at this passage.

Delight is the Hebrew word, "anag" which means to be soft or pliable. The word picture is indicative of the relationship of clay towards a potter. He puts the desire inside of your spirit when your heart becomes pliable in His hands. You have to let Him hold you and mold you, in order to accommodate the desires that He is putting in you. Now, understanding that whatever your desire is to do, it came from God. Realize He only places the desire after he has made room for His will in your life. In other words, He will cause you to thirst after His will. The awesome thing about really walking with the Lord is that the more we grow close to Him, the more we allow Him to place His desires within our spirit. I have never seen clay wrestle with the hands of a potter. But, often we want to wrestle with God and convince Him to fufill our desires and do what we want. It is only when we yield to His skillful hands, and trust in His power to do *in* us that which cannot be done *by* us, that we will see the manifestation of the desires of our heart.

I HAVE A DREAM

A quote from "I have a dream" by Dr. Martin Luther King, Jr. [Delivered on the steps of the Lincoln Memorial in Washington, D.C. on August 28, 1963]

"I say to you today, my friends, that in spite of the difficulties and frustrations of the moment, I still have a dream. It is a dream deeply rooted in the American dream.

I have a dream that one day this nation will rise up and live out the true meaning of its creed: "We hold these truths to be self-evident: that all men are created equal."

I have a dream that one day on the red hills of Georgia the sons of former slaves and the sons of former slaveowners will be able to sit down together at a table of brotherhood.

I have a dream that one day even the state of Mississippi, a desert state, sweltering with the heat of injustice and oppression, will be transformed into an oasis of freedom and justice.

I have a dream that my four children will one day live in a nation where they will not be judged by the color of their skin but by the content of their character.

I have a dream today.

I have a dream that one day the state of Alabama, whose governor's lips are presently dripping with the words of interposition and nullification, will be transformed into a situation where ***little black boys and black girls will be able to join hands with little white boys and white girls and walk together as sisters and brothers.***

I have a dream today.

> I have a dream that one day every valley shall be exalted, every hill and mountain shall be made low, the rough places will be made plain, and the crooked places will be made straight, and the glory of the Lord shall be revealed, and all flesh shall see it together."

This speech is one of the most powerful and significant pieces of literature in the history of our nation. Thirty-seven years ago Dr. Martin Luther King, Jr. stood looking into an uncertain future and prophesied to the racial injustice of our nation as he told "the dream." During the time of this speech, racism was at an all time high. There were places in America that could not be accessed by every American. Yet King dreamed. He dreamed of a day when we, as a nation, would stand together regardless of our skin color. Though his dream still has a way to go before it reaches complete and utter fulfillment, we are seeing evidence of it today. Let me show you the power of his vision. Twenty-seven years ago (ten years after Dr. King's speech), an African-American man from Shreveport, Louisiana met a Caucasian woman from Orfino, Idaho. The two of them fell in love, got married and had a son. You hold their son's book in your hand. What are you saying, Pastor Cain? That had it not been for the dream of a man thirty-seven years ago, I wouldn't be here today. I am the product of a dream and the dream lives on. You might ask, "What does this have to do with anything?" Don't let your dreams die. Don't let preconceived ideas, cultural limitations, traditions, fear, or intimidation rob you of your God-given dream. Don't let doubt and unbelief kill what the Lord has shown you. He placed the dream inside and He has every intention of seeing it come to pass. Hold the hand of the Dream-Maker and remember you have power with God!

I stand before you as a testimony that God-given dreams don't die. After it was all said and done, Joseph's brothers did bow before him. In the year 2001, white children are holding hands with black children all over our nation. And if you have not seen the manifestation of your dreams yet, don't give up because they too will come to pass.

Lord, if you didn't want me to have my dream then you wouldn't have shown it to me. Thank you that today the dreams that you have given me are coming to fruition in the name of Jesus.

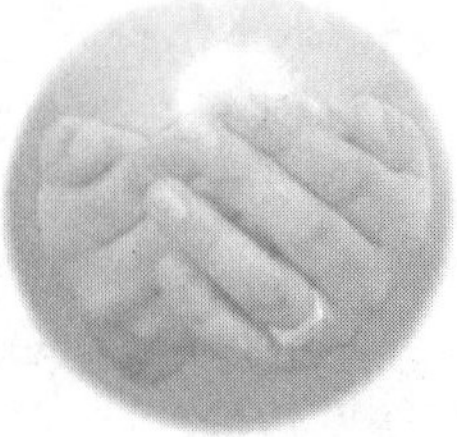

For verily I say unto you, That whosoever shall say unto this mountain, Be thou removed, and be thou cast into the sea; and shall not doubt in his heart, but shall believe that those things which he saith shall come to pass; he shall have whatsoever he saith.

—Mark 11:23

SEVEN

Talk Your Way Out

"And when he (the prodigal son) came to himself, he said..."

—Luke 15:17

THIS IS ONE OF THE MOST famous passages of Scripture, with regard to God's love towards the sinner. Although the story of the prodigal son dictates and reveals the heart of God concerning restoration, it also reveals the power of the spoken word. I'm afraid that few Christians truly understand the creative force that is released when we speak. Because we are created in the image and likeness of God, we have his creative attributes. Everything that God created was with a word. For, in the beginning God said, let there be light and there was light! Anytime God speaks, whatever comes out of his mouth must come to pass.

> *So shall my word be that goeth forth out of my mouth: it shall not return unto me void, but it shall accomplish that which I please, and it shall prosper in the thing whereto I sent it.*
>
> —Isaiah 55:11

And so it is with you. Whatever comes out of your mouth must come to pass! The problem is, we really don't believe that our words carry any significance, much less power. But, Jesus warned us of the danger of under-estimating the influence that our words have on our lives.

> *For by your words you will be acquitted, and by your words you will be condemned."*
>
> —Matthew 12:37

Because words are mere verbal expressions of thought, they are directly related to how you think. It was the prodigal son's thoughts that got him into trouble. He came to a place where he became discontented with his life and situation and he made the mistake of talking. Too often, we make the mistake of speaking too soon in a situation, or a circumstance, that we have become uncomfortable with. The Bible declares that this young man came to his father and said, "Give me my inheritance." That request was fostered by an attitude of greed and thanklessness.

Nonetheless, he asked for it and he got what he asked for. You know the rest of the story. He goes into a far land and begins to spend his money on what the Bible describes as riotous living. Sin will always take you where you really don't want to go, and it will make you pay more than what you had budgeted for. But, after disobedience and sin had run its course, the young man was reduced to an impoverished, desperate, ashamed and starving slave. While he is in the pigpen, knee-high in slop, he reached for a handful of what the pigs were eating. He was about to "dine with the swine," but suddenly, something happened. The Bible says that, "He came to himself," suggesting that all this time he was behaving out of character. He snapped back, realizing what he had done, where he was and what he was getting ready to do. I want you to notice very carefully what happened after he "came to himself."

> *But when he came to himself, he said, 'How many of my father's hired servants have bread enough and to spare, and I perish with hunger! I will arise and go to my father, and will say to him, "Father, I have sinned against heaven and before you…*
>
> —Luke 15:17-18 (NKJV)

Notice that when this young man came to himself, he began to speak. He opened his mouth right in the pigpen and, instead of putting something in it, he let something out of it. Right there, with the feeling of slime between his toes and the stench of filth around him, his spirit stood up within him and out from his lips came the statement, "I shall arise!"

Can I encourage you as you read this book? Can I tell you that there is still hope for what you are in right now? You might feel like there is no way out of the pigpen. You might think that you are facing insurmountable odds, but you have to understand the revelation that the prodigal son got right there, at the point of dining with the swine. He realized that it was what he had begun to say that had gotten him into the situation he was in, and if he could speak his way into it, then he could speak his way out! There is a miracle in your mouth. Stop cursing your finances with statements of lack and insufficiency, and "come to yourself." You might have spoken your way into that stage of your life, but surely you don't have to stay there. It is time to talk your way out. Begin to release faith in the spoken word of God and watch what will happen. The Bible teaches us that even God Himself has faith in His own word.

What I am trying to tell you is that God's word in your mouth is just as powerful as His word in His own mouth.

> *Through faith we understand that the worlds were framed by the word of God, so that things which are seen were not made of things which do appear.*
>
> —Hebrews 11:3

There has never existed a time when God doubted His word. When He has spoken, He has never once thought, "I wonder if this is going to work?" So, if God has faith in His own word, and we can see the manifestation of His word throughout creation, then if we have faith in His word, we will undoubtedly see the manifestation of His word in our personal lives.

What I am trying to tell you is that God's word in *your* mouth is just as powerful as His word in *His own* mouth.

MOVE THE MOUNTAIN

> *For assuredly, I say to you, whoever says to this mountain, 'Be removed and be cast into the sea,' and does not doubt in his heart, but believes that those things he says will be done, he will have whatever he says.*
>
> —Mark 11:23

Growing up in an old, traditional church, we used to sing a song: "I'm climbing up on the rough side of the mountain, and I'm doing my best to make it in." But, Jesus does not endorse or honor that type of mindset. The fact of the matter is, He never told us to climb any mountain. He said, "Speak to it!" Don't you understand? The miracle is in your mouth. All of heaven is waiting for you to open your mouth and articulate what the word of God has already declared. The angels are waiting to hear the word of God explode out of your mouth and lips. That mountain has stood tall and proud in your life for years, intimidating you and your family. It has told you what you would do, what you would have, and what you would never be able to accomplish. But, don't you think that it

There is a mountain mover in you. Speak to the mountain and command it, in the name of Jesus, to go jump in the lake and drown.

is about time to move that mountain? This is the day to give that heap of satanic obstacles its walking papers. It has got to go. There is a mountain mover in you. Speak to the mountain. Speak to the mountain of sickness and diseases. Speak to the mountain of depression. Speak to the dirty snowcaps of bondages in your life. Speak to the mountain of debt and lack, and command it, in the name of Jesus, to go jump in the lake and drown.

The words of faith that you dare to speak today will pave the way to your bright future tomorrow.

My beloved, you might have cursed yourself and created the mountains that now surround you, but it is not too late to put on your hard hat and begin to use the dynamite of God's word. Start leveling every mountain that stands in the way of the promise of God. Blow it up and move it out! Your faith is paving the way to your breakthrough. It's paving the way to your deliverance. The words of faith that you dare to speak today will pave the way to your bright future tomorrow. Your words, filled with faith, are going ahead of you and making the crooked places straight and the rough places plain.

SPEAK THE WORD ONLY

The centurion answered and said, "Lord, I am not worthy that You should come under my roof. But only speak a word, and my servant will be healed.

—Matthew 8:8 (NKJV)

The Roman centurion had initially requested that Jesus come and heal his servant, who was lying at the point of death. The Scriptures tell us that Jesus was en route when other servants of the centurion apprehended Him miles away from the house. I can imagine them in my mind, arriving huffing and puffing, bent over, holding their knees and trying to catch their breath. Finally, they get the news out. They tell Him that their master has relayed a word saying for Jesus not to come; that he feels unworthy of His presence, but to just "speak the word only" and it shall be done. In other words, do it by remote control. What he was saying was, just send through your words what you were personally going to deliver. He knew that Jesus' words could travel, no matter how far the distance. Jesus' eyes widened with surprise and He said.

> *Assuredly, I say to you, I have not found such great faith, not even in Israel!*
>
> —Matthew 8:10 (NKJV)

Then, the master cleared His throat and said, "let it be so." And the exact moment that He speaks the word, the centurion's servant begins to recuperate. If you are going to see the salvation of the Lord in every area of your life, you don't have time to speak everyone else's words. You don't need to know what other people say. You need to hear the eternal voice of God's word reverberate through your spirit. Thousands of years ago, God stood out on nothing and spoke a word saying, "Let there be light." Having said it once, His word went into a matrix cycle. That means, every day the sun shines and floods the earth with light, because that word God spoke continues to travel through the ions of space, time, and eternity. So when He said, "Let there be light," His word is so perpetual that what really came out of His mouth was, "Let there be LIGHT, LIGHT, LIGHT, LIGHT, LIGHT!" Here in the twenty-first century, there is still light and the sun still creeps over the horizon because His word reverberates through the universe. So it is with every promise He ever spoke.

This matrix cycle happens in your life when you agree with His word. So then, when you are sick in your body, it is no longer just

> *...By his stripes you were healed.*
>
> —1 Peter 2:24 (NKJV)

But now you hear it, "By His stripes you were HEALED, HEALED, HEALED, HEALED, HEALED. You hear,

> *And my God shall supply all your need according to His riches in glory by Christ Jesus.*
>
> —Philippians 4:19 (NKJV)

So now it sounds like, "My God shall SUPPLY, SUPPLY, SUPPLY, SUPPLY, SUPPLY ALL, ALL, ALL, ALL, ALL, your needs according to His RICHES, RICHES, RICHES, RICHES, RICHES in glory by Christ JESUS, JESUS, JESUS, JESUS, JESUS! It echoes within your heart and mind because every day when you wake up, there is a new and fresh resonating word for you. Stop speaking what He has not said about your finances. He never said that you were broke, so why do you say it? He never said that you would never have more than enough. So why have you concluded that this is all you will get out of life? He never said that you would have to borrow and be in debt. So, why have you just given up and resolved that this is the way it must be? Stop singing the blues and speak the word only. Send the word of God ahead of you into your work place and begin to exercise your faith, believing that God is elevating you within the company. Send the word ahead of you, thanking the Lord that He is supernaturally setting you up to go into business for yourself and you aren't going to have to go into debt or borrow any money to do it. The word of God prospers in everything that it is sent after. Read it again.

> *So shall My word be that goes forth from My mouth; It shall not return to Me void, But it shall accomplish what I please,* And it shall prosper in the thing for which I sent it.
>
> —Isaiah 55:11 (NKJV)

He said his word would prosper you. Make up your mind to stop speaking negatively over your finances, and over any other part of your life that you want to see changed. Make a vow to speak only what God says and you will see the power of His word begin to prosper you. He said that His word would not return void. He didn't say it wouldn't return. He said that it wouldn't return void. In other words, it won't come back empty-handed. Years ago, the Lord showed me that His word is like a boomerang. If you know anything about a boomerang, you know it was created as a hunting weapon. The hunter would sneak up on his prey and then direct and throw his boomerang. It would leave his hands rotating and spinning toward the animal. After disabling the prey it would return to the hands of the hunter, becoming his faithful companion of provision. That is what the Word of God must become to those of us who call on the name of the Lord. The word must become our "faithful companion of provision." As you aim it at the obstacle, release it with faith and authority, and watch it return to you having accomplished what it was sent to do. The word of God has traveled through time, generations, cultures, and continents simply to deliver to you what He has wanted you to have all along. So raise your hands right where you are and talk your way out!

> *Father God, I repent for cursing my life with my own words and mouth. Thank you for giving me the power to change my life with your word. Today I make a decision to speak the word only over my circumstances and I know that I will see your miraculous provision. I am going to get so full of your word that it will flow out of me whenever trouble comes.*

But this I say, He which soweth sparingly shall reap also sparingly; and he which soweth bountifully shall reap also bountifully.

—2 Corinthians 9:6

EIGHT

Reaping at the Speed of Light

I DON'T KNOW IF YOU REALIZE it or not, but it seems like the hours in the day have somehow been shortened. I remember, growing up, how long and well enjoyed our summer breaks used to be. I would get out of school and make a beeline to the local swimming pool with my swimming trunks in my backpack. I would spend my whole entire summer swimming and enjoying the sun bathe my small frame in her warm rays. There was something distinctly different about those times. Days were longer. It seemed as if everything I could possibly do or accomplish could easily get done within the margin of a day. Hours took their time in passing, no one was in a hurry to get anywhere or do anything, because there was always tomorrow. You might say that my recollection of time is the way it is because I was a child. But, I have talked to the elderly who were in the prime of their lives when I was a tike. They, too, agree that those were slower days, less stressful times and simpler generations. Now I am a father of three beautiful young rosebuds. Only yesterday, I held them in my arms as they lay so peacefully and undisturbed. Now two of them are in elementary school and the last one is asking every day for his chance. Just yesterday, I poured their milk and coached them to suck it out of the bottle I held. Now, they get their own milk, and Hershey's syrup is one of their good friends. Instead of getting up to get their milk, they beat me to it and, before I know what has happened, they are serving me chocolate milk that a professional bartender couldn't hold a candle to. I don't want them to grow up so fast. At times, I am afraid to fall asleep for fear that I will awake and years will have elapsed. I know that time doesn't stand still for anyone, but sometimes I think it would be nice to put it in slow motion. The day will come faster than I desire when my young rosebuds will no longer be buds at all but will blossom into breathtaking roses with their own rosebushes.

2000 AND BEYOND

As we have crossed over the threshold into a new millennium, time has put on its running shoes and has caught its second wind. Everyone is walking faster, talking faster, driving faster and living faster. We have DSLand cable lines that move the internet at speeds that are faster than ever, and assuredly, by the time you read this, there will be new technology that will make everything else before it look like we were driving Ms. Daisy.

If you have ever abused it, had a lack of appreciation for it, or taken it for granted, at some point or another you have also desired to kiss its feet and ask for it to walk backwards in your life. Yes, that's right, I'm talking about Time. When God created the world, He mapped out everything. He established everything that would ever happen and then gently placed it all within the perimeters of time. It has been said before, that God started at the end and then backed everything up to the beginning. Because He is Alpha and Omega, time cannot limit the Holy One of Israel.

There is stuff on reserve within your spirit: gifts, talents, revelation and power that your arch enemy had no idea were in you.

> *I am Alpha and Omega, the beginning and the ending, saith the Lord, which is, and which was, and which is to come, the Almighty.*
>
> —Revelation 1:8

One thing we must understand is that with God there is no succession of events. Because of His eternal quality, there is no distinction of past, present or future. In other words, in eternity, time does not exist, as we know time. The best way to explain eternity, then, would be to say that it is a "forever now." He established the perimeters of time for us, His creation, and from the beginning He set the rules.

> *While the earth remaineth, seedtime and harvest, and cold and heat, and summer and winter, and day and night shall not cease.*
>
> —Genesis 8:22

Here, the Lord shares the process of abundance. He explains that to every promise there is a process. Notice the succession of events. Seed, time and harvest. The first thing that must be noticed and introduced is the seed. A seed is a harvest in potential form. Everything that God begins, he starts in seed form. When He created the heavens and the earth, He commanded that everything would begin to produce after its own kind. When He created Adam and Eve, He said, "I'm not going to keep on coming down here and making mud pies and blowing bubbles into them. If you are going to get the next man you have to get him out of you".

This is the reason why the enemy has always been after the seed of man, his undeveloped potential. Because if the devil can stop you before you get started, his work is half done, but you have to understand that your seed is precious. There are things that God placed in you that you don't even know about. There is stuff on reserve within your spirit: gifts, talents, revelation and power that your arch enemy had no idea were in you. For had he known, he would have snuffed you out while you were in the world and he still had a chance.

The fact of the matter is, buried deep inside every seed is a forest screaming to get out. And given the proper conditions and care, that forest will explode from beyond the walls of that seed which had contained it. There is more inside of you than what is around you. No matter how much dirt separates a seed from the surface, it will eventually rise to the top. Regardless of how much "dirt" the enemy has tried to use to bury your God given potential, it too shall come forth.There is more inside of you than what has been on top of you. And your harvest is also grasping for the freedom to manifest in your life.

I'M STILL WAITING

Just today, my oldest son came in from school and showed me a little seed he had planted in a plastic cup. The little seedling had sprouted out of the soil and was beginning to grow. I instructed my son to put some water on it and put it outside so it could get some sunlight. After about fifteen minutes, he wanted to water it again, so I said, "Son you just watered it."

"I know Dad, but it's not growing," he said,

"Son, you will have to wait," I answered, "It will take time." Patience is the teacher of our faith. Often, we don't see the importance of waiting or its power. Because most of us are not farmers, when we use the example of a plant seed and an agricultural harvest, more often than not, we cannot relate to it. After all, if we need something to eat, we don't grow it, we go and buy it from the store, or stop by a drive through restaurant. But, maybe there is a better illustrative tool that could help us understand the process of seed-time-harvest and that is the relationship between the sperm and the egg. In II Corinthians 9:6-10, Paul says:

> *But this I say, He which soweth sparingly shall reap also sparingly; and he which soweth bountifully shall reap also bountifully. Every man according as he purposeth in his heart, so let him give; not grudgingly, or of necessity: for God loveth a cheerful giver. And God is able to make all grace abound toward you; that ye, always having all sufficiency in all things, may abound to every good work: (As it is written, He hath dispersed abroad; he hath given to the poor: his righteousness remaineth for ever. Now he that*

> *ministereth* seed *to the sower both minister bread for your food, and multiply your seed sown, and increase the fruits of your righteousness;)*
>
> —2 Corinthians 9:6-10

The Greek word for "seed" in verse ten is sperma, from which we get the English word "sperm." The Bible even teaches that the sperm is called the "seed" of man. When the sperm collides with the fertile egg, the egg is germinated and the beginning of life (conception) occurs. But, from the time that a woman gets pregnant to the time she gives birth to the child is a nine-month process. Some would even testify that it is a grueling process. Nonetheless, it is not an instant epiphany. It takes approximately nine months for this precious life to incubate, grow, and develop inside of the womb of its mother. While she is pregnant, the woman's anatomy begins to change. Her body begins to transform, altering to better accommodate the new creation inside of her. This is what we would call the "time." You cannot rush this process. You can't rush the growth or development of the child.

Oftentimes we try to rush the process of patience and miss out in the end because we receive a half-baked miracle instead of allowing God to maximize His glory in our circumstance.

The woman can only take care of herself, get a lot of rest, eat well, and pray until it is time for the baby to come out. Oftentimes we try to rush the process of patience and miss out in the end because we receive a half-baked miracle instead of allowing God to maximize His glory in our circumstance. So, if we understand it right, the formula is seed

+ time = harvest, faith + patience = promise, giving + waiting = financial breakthrough. Even though there are other specific things that play into this principle, the rudimentary ones are here: "seed-time-harvest." Now that I have spent all that time laying the foundation of this principle, get ready for the curve ball. About six months ago, the Lord began to deal with me concerning certain scriptures that I had been studying. I want to share them with you.

God is shortening the distance between you and your destiny, your purpose, your ministry and your dreams.

> *Behold, the days come, saith the Lord, that the plowman shall overtake the reaper, and the treader of grapes him that soweth seed; and the mountains shall drop sweet wine, and all the hills shall melt.*
>
> —Amos 9:13

We have crossed the threshold into a whole new era. This is the twenty-first century and I don't know if you are fully aware of what that means. God is speeding up the wheels of destiny and the Lord speaks through the mouth of his prophet saying "...The treader of the grapes, is going to overtake the sower..." In other words, God is saying that He is going to speed up the process of seed-time-and harvest.

The Lord told me to begin declaring to the body of Christ that it would no longer be seed-time-harvest like we knew it, but that He is taking time out of the equation. So, no longer is it seed time and harvest but now it is seed-harvest. If we, as the body of Christ, are going to accomplish what He has for us to do in this final hour, we must reap at the speed of light. Light travels at 188,000 miles per hour. We don't have the luxury of time anymore. Now is the time to release your faith and believe that before you can get your seed firmly planted in the ground, your harvest will be staring you in the face. The business that man took ten years to build will take you two. The plans that took five years to get implemented will take you five months in this new season. The promotion for you that took a year will now take a month, and those things that you would pace the floor at night thinking about, wondering if and when they would happen… oops they just did. God is shortening the distance between you and your destiny, your purpose, your ministry and your dreams. Time has been taken out of the equation, and now it is our time to get it all back. If you will begin to believe for immediate results when you give and pray, you will begin to see the threshold between you and your answer shortening right before your eyes. I have a news flash for you my brothers and sisters: It's your time! If, by chance, a religious skeptic has picked up this book, you haven't set it down yet because it is your time to begin to believe God is a right now God, a present help in time of need.

> *And it shall be, when the Lord thy God shall have brought thee into the land which he sware unto thy fathers, to Abraham, to Isaac, and to Jacob, to give thee great and goodly cities, which thou buildedst not, And houses full of all good* things, *which thou filledst not, and wells digged, which thou diggedst not, vineyards and olive trees, which thou plantedst not; when thou shalt*

> *have eaten and be full;* Then *beware lest thou forget the Lord, which brought thee forth out of the land of Egypt, from the house of bondage.*
>
> —Deuteronomy 6:10-12

You are getting ready to enjoy a whole new quality of life. This scripture proves that you are not going to be able to keep up with the blessings of God. As we have entered this new millennium, this seventh day, know it is the day of completion and rest.

> *And on the seventh day* God *ended his work which he had made; and he rested on the seventh day from all his work which he had made. And* God *blessed the seventh day, and sanctified it: because that in it he had rested from all his work which God created and made.*
>
> —Genesis 2:2-3

We are entering a season and dimension of rest that is going to scare the devil. Because you are not going to worry, stress or trip out anymore. When you begin to walk in this seventh day, you are going to notice that more is being done with less effort. Your workload will get lighter but the benefits will get greater.

> *Blessed* be *the Lord,* who *daily loadeth us* with benefits, even *the God of our salvation. Selah.*
>
> —Psalms 68:19

Listen very closely to me. There are some things that God is going to do for you that you aren't going to be able to contribute to good work ethics. As you rest in Him, they are going to come to you.

IS HE IN THE BOAT?

And when even was now come, his disciples went down unto the sea, And entered into a ship, and went over the sea toward Capernaum. And it was now dark, and Jesus was not come to them. And the sea arose by reason of a great wind that blew. So when they had rowed about five and twenty or thirty furlongs, they see Jesus walking on the sea, and drawing nigh unto the ship: and they were afraid. But he saith unto them, It is I; be not afraid. Then they willingly received him into the ship: and immediately the ship was at the land whither they went.

—John 6:16-21

This passage has been so powerfully amazing to me. This is not the same account of the storm in which Jesus was in the hinder part of the boat and He awakened and dispelled it. No, this account puts Him on the mountain. When Jesus saw them in trouble, He sets out on a three-mile stroll to get to where they were. But, this was not just any walk; he was walking on the water. He came to them supernaturally. So it was, when he saw us tossing and toiling on the sea of sin, He came to us. Wrapped in swaddling clothes and lying in a manger, He came to us. He came to us, clenched tightly in the arms of a scared virgin girl. He came, for thirty-three and a half years, just to get to where we were, so He could rescue us from our debauchery and sin. The Scripture says that as soon as they willingly received Him into the boat, they were immediately at their destination. They had left Tiberius and were trying to get to Capernaum. The two cities were across the sea of Galilee from each other, about six miles separating them. But, when Jesus stepped in the boat, that which would have taken most of the night was done in half the time. They were there before they knew it. When Jesus gets into something, it goes a whole lot faster! Has your business been dragging? Have your finances been slow? Has your profit margin been down? Do you find yourself in the middle of a financial storm? Give Jesus the helm of the ship and you will be surprised how fast things will change. Notice the scripture again. It didn't say they took there time getting there. It didn't say that they go there a little ahead of schedule. It doesn't even say that they got there fast. It says, "Immediately they were where they were going." Do something for me. Snap your fingers. Before you do it though, I want you to get ready to notice the time that will pass in that snap. All right, snap now! How fast was that? Immediately. That is how fast they were translated to the other side of the sea, and that is how fast you are going to arrive on the shore of your dreams when Jesus is in your boat. Stop saying, "one day I am going to reap the harvest of abundance that I have been sowing for." If the Master is in your boat, you have been approved to reap at the speed of light.

Father, I am so excited over how you are accelerating my harvest. Thank you that before I can get my seed firmly in the ground, my harvests are springing up all around me. Lord, I have determined in my heart to be a sower. To sow whenever the need arises and even when there is no "need." Because the more I sow the more I reap.

But seek first his kingdom and his righteousness, and all these things will be given to you as well.

—Matthew 6:33 (NIV)

NINE

Daddy, Look at Me

WHEN MY OLDEST SON WAS about three years old, he had gotten in the habit of climbing up in my lap whenever I would sit and talk with someone. He would sit and listen for a while, and then he would reach out with those pudgy toddler hands and grab me by both cheeks. He would turn my face directly into his and say very seriously, "Daddy, wook at me!" He would do this repeatedly until I looked directly into his eyes, then he would usually wrap his arms around my neck and say, "I wuv my Daddy!" In those moments, nothing could distract me from his voice! Whatever he needed, he got! If he wanted it, it was his! But, the fact

The expectation of our sowing should be an abundant harvest, but the motive for our giving must be the selfless love of a child for our Father!

was he really didn't want anything but me. My attention. My face. And because of that simple connection—the pure love of a child for his Daddy, the very best I could offer was his to receive. If we want to step up to the next level of God's blessing in our lives, we must shift our emphasis from His hands to His face! The *expectation* of our sowing should be an abundant harvest, but the *motive* for our giving must be the selfless love of a child for our Father! And the *method* of our giving must be soaked and wrapped in passionate worship! The highest, most intimate expression of worship is when we push aside His hands and pursue His face! *His face equals His favor!* In ancient cultures, to turn your face from someone meant to express disfavor with them. You were allowed in their presence, but refused their grace or favor. According to II Samuel 14, Absalom lived in Jerusalem for two years without being allowed to see his father, King David's face! It is possible to live in the kingdom and not see the King's face! You might enjoy all the protection a citizen of the kingdom is entitled to, but receive none of the favor of your King! We must approach Him just for Him, and not for what we can get out of Him — then the heart of our Father will melt toward us, His face will turn to us, and whatever we need will be poured upon us in abundance!

THE DOORKEEPER BLESSING

So many people spend their lives looking for life, afraid of what they might lose. They push and struggle to get ahead, constantly looking over their shoulder in fear or regret—letting their past dictate their future and corrupt their worship. For many, the "sacrifice of praise," focusing on God and His desires, rather than on us and our needs, is just too high a price to pay!

And then, there are people like Obed Edom.

Obed-Edom was a simple farmer, minding his own business when King David knocked on his door. "Greetings, Obed-Edom," said the king, "I have a favor to ask of you."

"Yes, sir, whatever the lord, my king, desires I will do!" replied Obed-Edom.

"It's not much, really. We just want to leave this box in your barn for a while…no big deal, right?" asked David.

"Well, I suppose not, but what kind of box is it? Why do you need to leave it here?" Obed-Edom inquired.

"Well, Obed-Edom, it's like this: we were taking the Ark of the Covenant to Jerusalem on this cart, see, and it started to tip over just up the road from your house. Well, one of my best men, Uzziah, reached out to steady the Ark, and…well…uhm…I guess he, uh—died. Soooo, anyway, we'll just leave that "box," the, uh, Ark of The Presence, with you, and we'll, uh, see-ya-later-bye!" the king said in a rush as he ran for Jerusalem.

Obed-Edom called out to his family, "Honey! Kids! We need to stay OUT of the barn for a while…."

Three months passed, and David heard that everything Obed Edom owned and everyone in his family had been outrageously blessed! God's presence had caused super-abundance to come to this simple farmer's family…but the story doesn't end there. David showed up at Obed-Edom's door again, this time to reclaim the

Ark and take it to Jerusalem correctly. The next time we hear about Obed-Edom and his family, they are living in Jerusalem, singing and playing in the praise team that surrounded the ark twenty-four hours a day! He and his family had abandoned their farm, and the blessed crops to stay close to the face of the Lord! And He continued to bless them there in Jerusalem. But, according to I Chronicles 16:38, Obed-Edom took a job as a janitor in the Tabernacle of David, where the Ark was. Now, you're probably thinking, what a demotion! From prosperous farmer to lowly janitor! But you must realize that Obed-Edom understood the truth of Psalm 84:10

> *Better is one day in your courts than a thousand elsewhere;*
> *I would rather be a doorkeeper in the house of my God than dwell in the tents of the wicked.*
> —Psalms 84:10 (NIV)

But, the story doesn't end there, either! To see what happened to Obed Edom and his children, you have to move forward several years to I Chronicles 26:8,15. These verses tell us that ALL sixty-two of his sons and grandsons were capable, strong, and skilled servants of God, well qualified for their work. *And they were put in charge of the storehouses of God!* In fact, over two hundred years later, Obed-Edom's family was in charge of all the gold, silver and vessels stored in the temple vault, as well as all the king's personal treasure!

Pursue His face and press into His presence, not for stuff, or needs, or blessings, but just for HIM — "...and all these things shall be added unto you."

Obed-Edom's children didn't rebel with the rest of Israel, and his inheritance grew and prospered both during his lifetime and throughout history, in spite of the famines and judgements on the local economy! And all this happened because he set his heart on God's face and refused to selfishly pursue His hands. Make a decision right now to cry out to God, "Look at me!" Pursue His face and press into His presence, not for stuff, or needs, or blessings, but just for HIM — "...and all these things shall be added unto you."

IT ISN'T LOVE UNTIL YOU GIVE IT

Paul concludes the twelfth chapter of I Corinthians with these words:

> *But covet earnestly the best gifts: and yet shew I unto you a more excellent way.*
>
> —1 Cor. 12:31

Love isn't love until you give it away. According to I Corinthians 13, the "more excellent way" is the way of love. Some Christians have misunderstood this statement to mean that we can seek God's love, or His gifts, but not both. But our God is a good Father who gives His best to His children. Jesus said as much in Matthew:

> *If ye then, being evil, know how to give good gifts unto your children, how much more shall your Father which is in heaven give good things to them that ask him?*
>
> —Matthew 7:11

And Paul made it clear that by giving His own Son, our heavenly Father demonstrated His willingness to give His best in all things:

> *If God didn't hesitate to put everything on the line for us, embracing our condition and exposing himself to the worst by sending his own Son, is there anything else he wouldn't gladly and freely do for us?*
>
> —Romans 8:32 (THE MESSAGE)

I understand His willingness and His eagerness to shower His children with blessings because of the intense, passionate love of a father's heart for his own. As a father, I love birthdays, holidays, Christmas…any excuse to give my children presents. Not because I want to add to their collection of stuff, or because they are in need, or to even satisfy their materialistic cravings. I love giving them things because my giving and their receiving draw us together in a moment of pure love and shared joy!

Our Father's best gifts are reserved for those who seek His presence more than His presents

Our Father's best gifts are reserved for those who seek His presence more than His presents, who pursue the giver more than the gift, and who worship the King, not the treasures of His Kingdom!

PASSION REQUIRED

To give out of a heart of love, rather than a selfish pursuit of gain, or an apathetic obligation to duty, requires passion!

According to the dictionary, passion is:

> *passion n 1: strong feeling or emotion 2: intense passion or emotion 3: something that is desired 4: an irrational but irresistible motive for a belief or action 5: any object of warm affection or devotion*

A man and his wife are shopping in a jewelry store. She "happens" to mention that their tenth wedding anniversary is coming up and, while it's not ***the*** diamond anniversary, it is ***a*** diamond anniversary. She also "happens" to mention that BEAUTIFUL diamond tennis bracelet and how much she's ALWAYS wanted one. Well, the husband, not being ***totally*** clueless, picks up on these subtle hints. However, that bracelet is expensive and he *really* wanted to buy that bass boat on sale at Wally's Fishing Emporium. But, he figures if he doesn't get the bracelet, he'll probably never hear the end of it and he'll feel guilty every time he goes fishing, which will ruin his whole season! So, muttering and frustrated, he goes back to the store and buys the bracelet. Their anniversary arrives and he walks into the bedroom before heading off to work.

He tosses the velvet box with the bracelet in it onto the bed and says, "Here. I know you wanted this, so I needed to buy it for you. Maybe now you won't mind cooking some steaks tonight for me? Gotta' go. See ya later. Oh, yeah…I love you—bye."

That husband's passionless, self-absorbed giving ruined the value of an eagerly anticipated gift and robbed his wife of any joy she might have had in receiving it! In the same way, our passionless, self-absorbed giving to God out of necessity or duty, ruins the value of our gifts and robs Him of the joy of our giving to Him!

Open your heart wide to Him right now! Ask Him to stir a passion for Him in your spirit greater than you've ever known! Make every gift you give, a gift from your heart to turn His face to you. Repent of self-absorbed, passionless giving and prepare to passionately, worshipfully, tenderly open your hand and give what is in it, that He might open the windows of heaven over you, your family, church, neighborhood and city. It's time to earnestly pursue the best gifts, the most excellent way! Are you an Obed Edom or an Absalom? A passionate pursuer of God's face or an opportunistic profit-seeker grabbing for His hands? Go ahead, pray it out loud in your own words right now:

"Daddy, wook at me!"

Daddy God, it is in your presence that there is joy forever more. I want to live looking at your face and not at your hands. I am more in love with you than I am with what you give me. Let it always be like that Lord and help me to always seek your Kingdom first in everything I say and do.

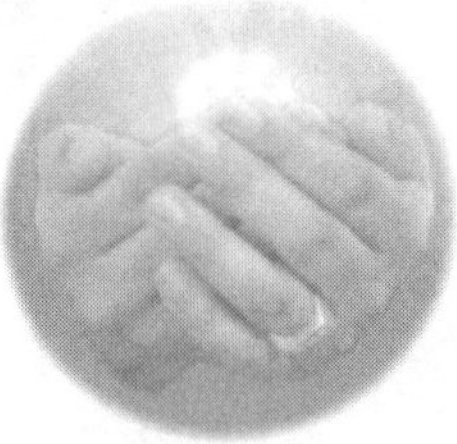

In the morning sow thy seed, and in the evening withhold not thine hand: for thou knowest not whether shall prosper, either this or that, or whether they both shall be alike good.

—Ecclesiastes 11:6

TEN

It's in Your Hand

And Moses answered and said, But, behold, they will not believe me, nor hearken unto my voice: for they will say, The LORD hath not appeared unto thee. And the LORD said unto him, What is that in thine hand? And he said, A rod. And he said, Cast it on the ground. And he cast it on the ground, and it became a serpent; and Moses fled from before it. And the LORD said unto Moses, Put forth thine hand, and take it by the tail. And he put forth his hand, and caught it, and it became a rod in his hand: That they may believe that the LORD God of their fathers, the God of Abraham, the God of Isaac, and the God of Jacob, hath appeared unto thee.

—Exodus 4:1-8

I think that if I were to pick a man in the Bible who overcame tremendous obstacles to walk in his God-given destiny, it would have to be Moses. This Hebrew boy couldn't get a break. He had a contract out on his life before he even got here. If you are going to receive the blessings that have already been prepared and ordained for you, you are going to have to realize there will be some struggles. When you understand that you have a date with destiny, you will also see that the greater the fight, the greater the call God has on your life. God allowed Moses to be born in Egypt, and to grow up the way He did, for the greater purpose. Egypt is the place of incubation. It is often in the place of struggle that God will grow the promise He gave you. He allowed the struggles you went through so it would produce within you a desire for better than what you were experiencing.

You might have walked away from some things, but nothing that you have ever walked away from will be able to compare with what you are in store for now.

The Bible states that it was Pharaoh's daughter who found Moses, but it is believed by many theologians to be her older sister who, according to Egyptian law, could not sit on the throne, yet whose seed would have the first right to the throne of Egypt. There was a problem, however. She was barren. Given that history, Moses should have been the next successor to the throne. It was Ramsey II that occupied the seat of Pharaoh when Moses returned to Egypt. Moses could go back into

Egypt without intimidation because he saw a pharaoh sitting on a throne, that should and would have been his had he not left Egypt. It is also the reason why the power of temptation can no longer can hold you. Because you can walk away from that when God shows you this. I want to let you know that you might have walked away from some things, but nothing that you have ever walked away from will be able to compare with what is in store for you now.

It is not certain when Moses got his rod, but it is certain where. He found his rod in his wilderness. The place of his seclusion, his loneliness and frustration is the same place where God gave Moses His commission, and showed him what He would use to bring it to pass. God had brought him to this place to deal with him and to remove all other support, so that Moses would have no one else to trust except God Himself. When Moses noticed the bush that was burning and yet not being consumed, the Bible says that he turned aside to see it. He had to get off the mainstream path and view God in a light that he had never seen him before. God is saying to us, "If you are going to see the manifestation of my power in your life, you are going to have to stop looking at man. Because it's going to take the Me within you, to believe the Me outside of you, telling you that I am going to fulfill My promise to you. It is going to take you believing that I have given you enough to do, what I have called you to do." God always uses the least likely means to bring about His Master Design. And it is not going to be the thing that you don't have that is going to be the key. It's going to be the thing that you thought all along wasn't enough.

For Moses, that blessing was a rod. For Joshua, it was a spear. Samson's river of refreshing came from the jawbone of an ass. Powerful miracles and deliverances were transferred by simple handkerchiefs and aprons placed on Paul's body. It was Peter's shadow, the widow of Zeraphath's last meal and oil. It was Elijah's mantle, the little lad's two fish and five loaves of bread. It was David's rock and a rag, and for you, it will be the very thing that you have, that you thought God could never use.

PUT IT ALL IN HIS HANDS

Thou shalt also be a crown of glory in the hand of the Lord, and a royal diadem in the hand of thy God.

—Isaiah 62:3

In just a couple of minutes you will have concluded reading this last chapter. You will possibly set this book down, never to pick it up again, or possibly put it away to read again at a later date, or even better, pass it on to a friend who is struggling. But, before another minute passes, you need to decide that you are going to live in the radiant light of the blessings of God. I wrote this book to provoke you to faith, to mess with your mindset and make you doubt the life of defeat and mediocrity that you may have been living. I dare you to dream your dream and live it out to the fullest. But, please understand that even though the Lord has blessed you, He is the only one who can maintain it.

In the book of I Samuel, there is the story of a woman name Hannah. Her womb had been shut up and she faced daily persecution and provocation from her rival. The Bible declares that Hannah came into the house of the Lord and made a vow to God. There is a lot to be said for vows, but that is another book. What should be noted is that God honored His end of the deal by giving Hannah the son that she so desperately desired. And she honored hers too, by giving the lad back to God as she had promised she would. The boy didn't belong to Hannah. For nine months Hannah carried the Lord's child, because she had given him back to God. What I am trying to say is, if God can trust that you will put it in His hands, He will bless you beyond measure. She gave the Lord a little boy, but God gave Israel a prophet. Today is the day and now is the time for you to enter into the season of God's supernatural provision for you. You see, everyone who ever did something worth recording and retelling, was not noted because they were exceptionally talented. At least they didn't think they were. But, there was something they had determined that they would never be, and that is ordinary. If you are going to be exceptional in whatever your assignment is, you are going to have to decide that you are an exceptional person. You are going to have to fight, and beat off, the grasp of ordinary that will try and rap its ugly hands around your neck. The enemy of exceptional is ordinary, and the last thing that you are is ordinary. You, my friend, are a work of art.

What God is going to do for you is not coming from above you, but from within you.

> *For we are God's masterpiece. He has created us anew in Christ Jesus, so that we can do the good things he planned for us long ago.*
>
> —Ephesians 2:10 (NLT)

There are things in you that only you will ever be able to do. No one is like you. No one has your fingerprint. No one has your DNA. You are unique, and according the word of God, you are His masterpiece. The blessing of your life will commence when you start to realize that what God is going to do for you is not coming from above you, but from within you. And the worst thing you could do is to judge your success based on someone else's accomplishments. You are not anyone else and I guarantee you that no one else is you. Why would you want to be a cheap copy, when you can be a great original? Just be the best you that you can be. If you will just be yourself, you will be in a league all by yourself. I dare you to do one of the most frightening things that you will ever do. Because, as great as your blessing is, it still won't be enough until you give it to the Master of multiplication. You might say, "Well, I just don't see what I have that God would use." I guess it all depends on whose hand it's in. See, a basketball in my hand costs about thirty dollars. But a basketball in Michael Jordan's hand is worth about thirty million dollars. A football in my hand is worth maybe forty dollars, but a football in Emmitt Smith's hand is worth forty million dollars. A golf club in my hand is an embarrassment, but a golf club in Tiger Wood's hand is championship after championship. A pen in my hand is just a couple of notes, but a pen in Shakespeare's hand is Hamlet, and Romeo and Juliet. A peanut in my hand is just a nice snack, but a peanut in George Washington Carter's hands is peanut butter, it's hair grease, it's shampoo and hair conditioning. It just all depends on whose hand it is in. A nail in my hand is just a couple of minor repairs, but a nail in Jesus' hand is the salvation of the world!

As great as your blessing is, it still won't be enough until you give it to the Master of multiplication.

When Moses went back into Egypt to relay the message that God had instructed him to give Pharaoh, he experienced tremendous opposition. But, after it was all said and done, he stood on the banks of the Red Sea with the multitudes the Lord had delivered and brought out. Yet, even there in that place He had forgotten what God had given him.

> *And the Lord said unto Moses, Wherefore criest thou unto me? Speak unto the children of Israel, that they go forward: But lift thou up thy rod, and stretch out thine hand over the sea, and divide it: and the children of Israel shall go on dry ground through the midst of the sea.*
>
> —Exodus 14:15-16

Their deliverance was directly connected to what was in Moses' hand. Had he not used what was in his hand, they would all have died by the sword of the Egyptians. God asked Moses, "Why are you crying to me? Why are you telling these people that I am going to do something? Didn't I already give you what you need for this journey? You get up and divide the sea." And that is what the Lord is telling you. You have the right stuff. You've got what it takes. Although there was a wilderness that awaited them on the other side of that sea, and there they would have to learn to trust God even more, to cross this sea meant to leave all the debt and bondage of Egypt behind. Don't you think it is time that you made that same trip? I saw something for the first time ever, just today, as I read this passage of Scripture. Moses told the people to stand still and see the salvation of the Lord in verse fourteen. But God told Moses to tell the people to go forward in verse sixteen. God wasn't telling the children of Israel to stand still and He is not telling you that either. No, He is saying, "Go forward!" Don't stay in debt. Don't stay in a spirit of poverty and lack. Don't stay in depression. Don't stay in sickness and disease. Don't stay in small thinking, but go forward. Go forward into your wealthy place. Go forward into your land that flows with milk and honey. Go forward into your healing, your deliverance, your breakthrough. The Lord has not told you to camp out here. Don't wait for things to change before you advance ahead. Walk in faith and dominion.

Square your shoulders, straighten your back, quicken your step and, in the name of Jesus, lift your hand and watch the waters roll out of your way. The next time the devil, circumstances, or even people tell you that you don't have what it takes to be blessed, just cup your hands in front of them and with a chuckle in your voice say, "Too late to tell me that, because it's already in my hand."

The Blessing is in Your Hands
Order Form

Postal orders: W. E. Cain Ministries
P.O. Box 920
Hurst, TX 76053

Telephone orders: (817) 282-1077

Please send *The Blessing is in your Hands* to:

Name: ______________________________________

Address: ____________________________________

City: _______________________ State: ________

Zip: __________

Telephone: (_____) ________________

Book Price: $12.00

Shipping: $3.00 for the first book and $1.00 for each additional book to cover shipping and handling within US, Canada, and Mexico. International orders add $6.00 for the first book and $2.00 for each additional book

Or order from:

ACW Press
5501 N. 7th. Ave. #502
Phoenix, AZ 85013

(800) 931-BOOK

or contact your local bookstore